IBM Worklight Mobile Application Development Essentials

Develop efficient mobile applications using IBM Worklight

Muhammad Saif Uddin

Talha Haroon

BIRMINGHAM - MUMBAI

IBM Worklight Mobile Application Development Essentials

First published: February 2014

Production Reference: 1140214

Published by Packt Publishing Ltd.
Livery Place
35 Livery Street
Birmingham B3 2PB, UK.

ISBN 978-1-78217-760-9

www.packtpub.com

Cover Image by Ronak Dhruv (ronakd@packtpub.com)

Credits

About the Authors

Muhammad Saif Uddin has diverse experience in mobile, software, and web development. For the past few years, he has been exploring new mobile development environments to make mobile app development easy in the future. He has exposure to most of the development technologies that exist but is mainly focused on Android and iOS mobile development. He has successfully designed over 30 mobile apps, which are distributed on iTunes and App Store — AMEX Mobile and Bayt Mobile are two of these apps. He is also IBM Worklight Certified, and besides his remarkable knowledge of the mobile world, he has introduced many enterprise and web applications with Responsive Web Design. He blogs at `http://saifo.blogspot.com` and writes articles and tutorials on different technologies that include Android, Worklight, and Java. He lives in Karachi, Pakistan, with his wife and family.

First, I would like to thank Almighty Allah (Subahana wa tala). The people I'd like to thank most for their direct or indirect help in writing this book are my wife and my parents; the rest of my family for their love and support; and my fellow staff and friends who gave me encouragement and support, including Adeel Ansari, Aneel Ansari, Kashif Haseeb, Babar Qadri, and Mobin Khan.

Finally, I'd like to thank my co-author, Talha Haroon, without whom this project wouldn't have been possible.

Talha Haroon initially started working in the HRM and CRM fields as his main areas of focus, but later on in his career path, he dedicatedly moved to MobileFirst. If we glance at his specialities, then it would become apparent that he has proficient expertise in ERP's development and customization as well as mobile hybrid development. He is also IBM Worklight Certified and has deployed and developed many enterprise and mobile applications in which AMEX Mobile app and `AppleVacationsOnline.com` are the most highlighted and his biggest products. Moreover, he has introduced some futuristic business processes that will assist retail businesses to grow by themselves.

After thanking Allah (subahana wa tala), I am pleased to thank my mother, Fauzia Haroon, who always prays for me and has made me capable enough to raise myself in an upright way. Of course, my special thanks to my co-author, Muhammad Saif Uddin, who played a very crucial role within this project.

Acknowledgement

The staff at Packt Publishing worked inexhaustibly with us to make sure that this book attained the level of quality that we hoped for, and we thank them for their efforts. Without them, this book would not have been possible. It includes not only our publisher, but also the following contributors: Priyanka Shah, Jomin Varghese, Ashish Bhanushali, and fellow reviewers include ABDUL AHAD, Houcem BERRAYANA, Touchapon Kraisingkorn, Mohammad Omer Raza, and Saurabh Srivastava.

Special thanks to Mustafa Qutbuddin, CEO, Royal Cyber. It was because of you that we were able to get this book completed.

Also, special thanks to Syed Basheer, Senior Manager, Royal Cyber, for playing your part and providing perfect guidance to us.

About the Reviewers

ABDUL AHAD is a senior consultant with 10 years' IT experience. He has worked on different platforms, technologies, and tools. He has excellent skill sets and knowledge on IBM and mobility solutions. He works in a premier business partner company of IBM.

Houcem BERRAYANA is a senior Java software developer. Because he works in the IT services domain, he has had the chance to work on many technologies and domains such as JEE, Android, Worklight, PHP, and Rails. And he has experience in dealing with different kinds of clients such as banks, telecom operators, startups, and big companies. He loves web development and always prefers designing the backend of an application. He started using the hybrid mobile application in 2010.

He has already delivered three Worklight projects, and one of them is considered as one of the biggest Worklight deployments until now. He was designing the details of both JavaScript and server-side implementations.

He works at Proxym-IT, a very cool Tunisian IT company, providing IT services and works for cool projects and technologies.

> I would like to thank my wife for being patient during all the difficult moments we've encountered so far. I can never forget the support I've received from my mother and father all this while.

Touchapon Kraisingkorn is an IBMer who's worked with IBM Worklight since its acquisition. He's experienced in HTML5 and cross-platform development. Six years of HTML5 experience and five years of Java programming experience allows him to deeply understand how Worklight works under the hood.

Worklight is wildly popular in IBM, Thailand, and IBM has made it clear that mobile platform is one of its main focuses.

Mohammad Omer Raza is a graduate with a Bachelor of Computer Science and Information Technology from NED University. He started his career as a software engineer of mobile solutions. With his experience, he was able to complete the IBM Worklight certification, which was one of his greatest achievements at an early stage. Working on the highly rated AMEX Mobile app was a great test and milestone. Besides working on IBM Worklight, he has been working on different technologies such as PhoneGap, Titanium, and so on. He opted for a career in mobile development when he was in his final year of graduation after selecting an Android app as his final year project. For this project, he received the second highest score in his class. He was among the top 20 individuals, out of 100 who participated in Incubator 2012. He was selected for his project, which gave him a strong indication that mobile development was the career path he was looking for. He has started blogging on `http://omerhw.blogspot.in/`.

I would like to thank Almighty Allah for all his blessings on me and then would like to thank my dad, late Mohammad Raza Siraj; without his efforts, I wouldn't have been where I am today.

My thanks to the authors who wrote this book, Muhammad Saif Uddin and Talha Haroon; the staff of Packt Publishing; and contributors Priyanka Shah and Jomin Varghese who worked dedicatedly in completing this book with the best lines in it and gave me the opportunity to review the code of the material.

Special thanks to Mustafa Qutbuddin, CEO, Royal Cyber; Syed Basheer, Senior Manager, Royal Cyber; and ABDUL AHAD, Project Manager, Royal Cyber.

Saurabh Srivastava leads User Experience and HCI initiatives in IBM India Research Lab. His area of research includes the development of bottom-of-pyramid communities, speech interfaces, gestural interactions, information visualization, intelligent user interfaces, audio integration methods, and tangible media. As far as IBM research goes, he is part of the Telecom Research Group and focuses to deliver mobile-enabled solutions for emerging markets.

He has authored many publications in scientific conferences and journals. He is an active onboard member of the reviewing committee of reputed conferences and has chaired multiple ACM/IEEE workshops. He has been invited for talks and lectures in reputed institutes across the world.

He graduated from the Indian Institute of Technology, Bombay.

I would like to thank the entire Packt Publishing team for a smooth and insightful review process. A huge thanks to Jomin Varghese for his support and patience throughout. Also, sincere thanks to Nishanth for giving me the opportunity to examine this thoughtful piece of work.

A special thanks to Ketki, my wife, for understanding me during those weekends when I was busy with the book instead of sharing house chores and my time with her.

www.PacktPub.com

Support files, eBooks, discount offers and more

You might want to visit www.PacktPub.com for support files and downloads related to your book.

Did you know that Packt offers eBook versions of every book published, with PDF and ePub files available? You can upgrade to the eBook version at www.PacktPub.com and as a print book customer, you are entitled to a discount on the eBook copy. Get in touch with us at service@packtpub.com for more details.

At www.PacktPub.com, you can also read a collection of free technical articles, sign up for a range of free newsletters, and receive exclusive discounts and offers on Packt books and eBooks.

http://PacktLib.PacktPub.com

Do you need instant solutions to your IT questions? PacktLib is Packt's online digital book library. Here, you can access, read, and search across Packt's entire library of books.

Why Subscribe?

- Fully searchable across every book published by Packt
- Copy and paste, print, and bookmark content
- On demand and accessible via a web browser

Free Access for Packt account holders

If you have an account with Packt at www.PacktPub.com, you can use this to access PacktLib today and view nine entirely free books. Simply use your login credentials for immediate access.

Instant Updates on New Packt Books

Get notified! Find out when new books are published by following @PacktEnterprise on Twitter, or the *Packt Enterprise* Facebook page.

Table of Contents

Preface

IBM Worklight provides an open, comprehensive, and advanced mobile enterprise application platform that anticipates what developers need to develop, run, and manage HTML 5, hybrid, and native for smartphones and tablets in an easier and more efficient manner. *IBM Worklight Mobile Application Development Essentials* introduces you to Worklight right from setting up the environment using Eclipse to guiding you through the major features and techniques.

What this book covers

Chapter 1, Getting Started with IBM Worklight, is an introduction to Worklight and where it fits in with the IBM Mobile Application Platform. At the end of this chapter, you will understand the basic components of the IBM Worklight product and how it contributes to building a mobile application.

Chapter 2, Installing Worklight, is about getting Worklight up and running for development on your computer. At the end of this chapter, you will have a Worklight environment on your machine. This will enable you to work through the remaining chapters and build Worklight applications even on Android.

Chapter 3, Creating a Basic Worklight Application, is about creating a Worklight application from scratch. At the end of this chapter, you will have created a default empty Worklight application and will understand how to view in the simulator supplied with Worklight.

Chapter 4, Customizing the Worklight Application, is about adding basic content to a Worklight application to customize the Dojo component to achieve native functionality and using local test data. Moreover, this chapter covers adding Worklight environments to a Worklight application, which allows different mobile platforms to be supported. At the end of this chapter, you will know how to add Dojo mobile-based web content to your Worklight application using the graphical tools and different mobile platforms supported by Worklight and how to add the Android environment to an application.

Chapter 5, Adding an Adapter, is about Worklight Adapters and how they can be used to integrate client applications with backend data services.

Chapter 6, Authentication and Security, will give you extensive information about the authentication frameworks and security module of IBM Worklight. This chapter covers basic, form-based, adapter-based, and custom authentication. After going through this chapter, you will be armed with the knowledge and confidence to develop your own authentication and set up efficient security measures in your developed application.

Chapter 7, Advanced Features of IBM Worklight, covers native development for the Android platform including some advanced subjects for web-optimized and hybrid pages. Push notification with complete understanding and process cycles are derived to understand its mechanism. Worklight API implementation with process handling is the most critical part to define. But, proper functional behavior is revealed to make it's understanding much easier.

What you need for this book

You will need the following software for this book:

- Eclipse Juno 4.2.2 (Java Platform, Enterprise Edition, or Classic).
- IBM Worklight Studio Plugin Developer Edition (it's free and it runs completely within eclipse; there's no standalone Worklight server). (If you've installed a separate Worklight server—on Liberty, WAS, or Tomcat—you're running the Worklight Consumer or Worklight Enterprise Edition and should use the studio plugin for that edition/version. Business partners can get the corresponding studio plugin from PartnerWorld.)
- The Android ADT Plugin for eclipse and Android SDK.

Who this book is for

If you are a mobile developer, from a novice to a more advanced level, who wants to create a cross-platform app using IBM Worklight, this book is ideal for you.

All novice and expert web developers who wish to learn mobile application development with a minimum experience in technologies such as HTML, CSS, and JavaScript will benefit from this book.

IBM Worklight leverages you to create highly interactive and usable mobile applications with the help of the concepts and code exercises defined from chapter to chapter. With the exercises, you immediately put your learning to work. Moreover, this book covers the popular UI frameworks demonstrated using Worklight such as jQuery mobile and Dojo framework.

Both the novice and experienced users will benefit greatly from this book and add this knowledge to their toolbox quickly.

Conventions

In this book, you will find a number of styles of text that distinguish between different kinds of information. Here are some examples of these styles, and an explanation of their meaning.

Code words in text are shown as follows: "We can include other contexts through the use of the `include` directive."

A block of code is set as follows:

```
<div id="AppBody">
  <div id="header">
  <div id="wrapper"> Welcome </div>
  </div>
  Hello World
</div>
```

When we wish to draw your attention to a particular part of a code block, the relevant lines or items are set in bold:

```
[default]
exten => s,1,Dial(Zap/1|30)
exten => s,2,Voicemail(u100)
exten => s,102,Voicemail(b100)
exten => i,1,Voicemail(s0)
```

New terms and **important words** are shown in bold. Words that you see on the screen, in menus or dialog boxes for example, appear in the text like this: "Click on **Install New Software** in the **Help** menu."

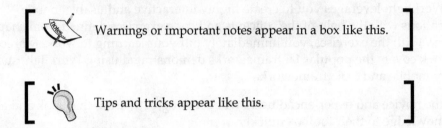

Warnings or important notes appear in a box like this.

Tips and tricks appear like this.

Reader feedback

Feedback from our readers is always welcome. Let us know what you think about this book—what you liked or may have disliked. Reader feedback is important for us to develop titles that you really get the most out of.

To send us general feedback, simply send an e-mail to feedback@packtpub.com, and mention the book title via the subject of your message.

If there is a topic that you have expertise in and you are interested in either writing or contributing to a book, see our author guide on www.packtpub.com/authors.

Customer support

Now that you are the proud owner of a Packt book, we have a number of things to help you to get the most from your purchase.

Downloading the example code

You can download the example code files for all Packt books you have purchased from your account at http://www.packtpub.com. If you purchased this book elsewhere, you can visit http://www.packtpub.com/support and register to have the files e-mailed directly to you.

Errata

Although we have taken every care to ensure the accuracy of our content, mistakes do happen. If you find a mistake in one of our books—maybe a mistake in the text or the code—we would be grateful if you would report this to us. By doing so, you can save other readers from frustration and help us improve subsequent versions of this book. If you find any errata, please report them by visiting http://www.packtpub.com/submit-errata, selecting your book, clicking on the **errata submission form** link, and entering the details of your errata. Once your errata are verified, your submission will be accepted and the errata will be uploaded on our website, or added to any list of existing errata, under the Errata section of that title. Any existing errata can be viewed by selecting your title from http://www.packtpub.com/support.

Piracy

Piracy of copyright material on the Internet is an ongoing problem across all media. At Packt, we take the protection of our copyright and licenses very seriously. If you come across any illegal copies of our works, in any form, on the Internet, please provide us with the location address or website name immediately so that we can pursue a remedy.

Please contact us at copyright@packtpub.com with a link to the suspected pirated material.

We appreciate your help in protecting our authors, and our ability to bring you valuable content.

Questions

You can contact us at questions@packtpub.com if you are having a problem with any aspect of the book, and we will do our best to address it.

1
Getting Started with IBM Worklight

The mobile industry is evolving rapidly with an increasing number of mobile devices, such as smartphones and tablets. More people are accessing services via mobile devices than ever before. The mobile solution is directly impacting businesses, organizations, and their growing number of customers and partners. Even employees now expect to access services on a mobile device.

This chapter is an introduction to Worklight and where it fits into IBM Mobile Application Platform. At the end of this chapter, the reader will understand the basic components of IBM Worklight and how it contributes to building mobile applications. Currently, there are several approaches for mobile application development, such as the following:

- **Web development**: This approach uses open web client programming modules, such as HTML5 and JavaScript.

- **Hybrid development**: This approach uses the app source code that consists of the web code, executed within a native container that is provided by Worklight and native libraries.

- **Hybrid mixed**: The developer adds arguments to the web code using the native language to create unique features and access native APIs that are available via JavaScript, such as APIs for a camera, an accelerometer, and other functionalities.

- **Native development**: In this approach, the application is developed using native languages or transcoded into a native language via MAP tool's native appearance device capabilities, and performance.

To develop a similar application on a different platform requires a different level of expertise, which is expensive in terms of cost, time, and complexity. The following table outlines the major aspects of the different approaches to development. Reviewing this list can help you choose the approach that is ideal for your particular mobile application.

	Native	Hybrid	Mobile Web
Skills/tools	• Objective C • Java	• HTML5 • CSS3 • JavaScript • Client-side frameworks	• HTML • CSS • JavaScript
Distribution	App store	App store	Internet/online
Development speed	Slow	Moderate	Fast
Device accessibility	Full native device access	Full native device access	Partial device access
Application maintenance	Difficult	Moderate	Easy

The hybrid development approach is about taking advantage of both native and mobile web development approaches. It benefits from the versatility of web technologies combined with powerful device features and SDK. It is well suited for a range of applications and can still provide good user experience.

The following table highlights the advantages and disadvantages of the hybrid approach:

Advantages of the hybrid approach	Disadvantages of the hybrid approach
Lower learning curve	Performance of the application is slightly slower than native approach because of the data access across multiple layers
Fast to develop and release	
Easy to port, making it cost effective	
Access to and support for native device functionality	

When escalating the business perspective to the mobile platform, we need to build an application for web-based responsive mobile apps with rich development environment for better performance and vast access control. IBM Worklight seems to be the most efficient and optimized to handle any kind of interactive and enterprise mobile application. Generally, the hybrid solutions are dependent on less secure or custom security identifiers, but Worklight's built-in security modules provides perfectly improvised frameworks to implement. Besides all of its classified and highly efficient features, it provides a complete studio to implement rich application development. For server-side security and implementation, it provides complete console management and accessibility for every component. It can also be utilized for creating a report and generating a complete view to study application statistics and performance. If you merge all cross-platforms into one, then IBM Worklight will be much trusted and efficient to use for business modernization and management.

IBM Worklight is an extensible mobile application platform that brings together many mobile capabilities into a single product and allows organizations to develop and deliver HTML5, hybrid and native applications, and deliver these applications with mobile middleware, security features, integrated data management, and analytics capabilities.

The IBM Worklight solution

In 2012, IBM acquired its very first set of mobile development and integration tools called IBM Worklight, which allows organizations to transform their business and deliver mobile solutions to their customers. IBM Worklight provides a truly open approach for developers to build an application and run it across multiple mobile platforms without having to port it for each environment, that is, Apple iOS, Google Android, Blackberry, and Microsoft Windows Phone. IBM Worklight also makes the developer's life easier by using standard technologies such as HTML5 and JavaScript with extensions for popular libraries such as jQuery Mobile, Dojo Toolkit, and Sencha Touch.

IBM Worklight offers an open platform to assist businesses to deliver existing and new mobile applications to multiple devices. According to IBM, "*it is an important piece of IBM's strategy*" that simplifies end-to-end security and service integration between mobile applications and backend systems. Additionally, it helps clients dramatically reduce mobile application time to market, cost, and complexity. Moreover, IBM Worklight came up with variety of components to efficiently develop, test, connect, run, and manage mobile applications.

The following screenshot summarizes the capabilities, extensive frameworks, and tools within Worklight:

Worklight capabilities and supported platforms

A relative newcomer to this world of cross-platform development, Worklight has dramatically taken its place within the community. IBM Worklight aims to change the way in which mobile developers think about creating rich functionality in their mobile applications. It does this in a very efficient manner, providing a complete platform for development unlike other cross-platform developers who only offer libraries to do the job.

Development in IBM Worklight is similar to web development, where developers and designers can leverage their existing knowledge of **Cascading Style Sheet (CSS)**, **Hypertext Markup Language (HTML)**, and straightforward JavaScript to manipulate pages and their elements directly, making development more rapid. The IDE works in conjunction with the native SDKs while building an app for Android.

The IDE builds and compiles the Android project and exports it within the same IDE. For iPhone, it generates files for an Xcode project.

In this book, we're going to take an in-depth look at what Worklight has to offer for building rich mobile applications. Let's start by finding out what exactly Worklight brings to the mobile development environment.

Components of Worklight

IBM Worklight is a mobile application platform containing all of the tools needed to develop a mobile application. If we combine IBM Worklight components into a stream, it would be clean to say that hybrid mobile application development is tightly coupled with a baseline.

Each component in Worklight is integrated with the other, for the creation of a rich interface and cost-effective mobile app in fragments, and to control the growing portfolio of an application. IBM Worklight provides high user experience index and full device access with native controls. It is a mobile application development tool that contains all modules, including the mobile application development framework and modules for testing and distribution. There are mainly two development editions:

- IBM Worklight Enterprise Edition
- IBM Worklight Consumer Edition

IBM Worklight Enterprise and Consumer Editions are identical except for the licensed models. The Consumer Edition is completely licensed per mobile application, whereas the Enterprise Edition contains license per device.

Every specified component provides a bundle of functionalities and support. The following is the lifecycle for mobile application development:

- **Worklight Studio**: IBM Worklight provides a robust, Eclipse-based development environment called Worklight Studio, which allows developers to quickly construct mobile applications for multiple platforms.

- **Worklight Server**: This component is a runtime server that activates or enables secure data transmission through centralized backend connectivity with adapters. It is used for offline encrypted storage, unified push notification, and many other applications.

- **Worklight Device Runtime**: The device runtime provides a rich set of APIs that are accessible across platforms and offer easy access to the services provided by the IBM Worklight Server.

- **Worklight Console**: This is a web-dependent interface for real-time analytics, managing push notification authority, and mobile version management. Worklight Console is a web-based interface and is dedicated to ongoing administration of Worklight Server and its deployed apps, adapters, and push notification services.

- **Worklight Application Center**: This is a cross-platform mobile application store that fulfils specific needs for mobile application development teams.

Each component is discussed in detail in the following sections.

Worklight Studio

IBM Worklight Studio provides a complete extensible environment with maximum code reusability and device optimization. It contains client-side implementation and web technologies that rely on the Worklight optimization framework. In this component, a user can find third-party library integration with device SDKs. The main purpose of this module is to create a hybrid application that can be used on and is deployable to any mobile platform such as Android, iPhone, Blackberry, and Windows Phone.

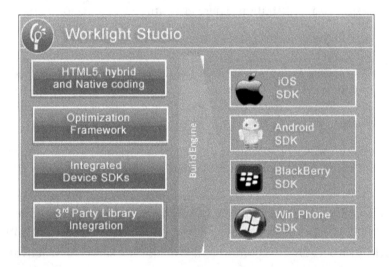

Features of the Worklight Studio platform

The preceding screenshots illustrates the Worklight Studio. It's an Eclipse-based IDE to facilitate the developer with operating and controlling projects in a normal hierarchical structure and to organize the source code for easy access. It is responsible for code maintenance, framework implementation, and rich multiplatform development. It also contains a variety of procedures to achieve device portability.

We will explore the key functionality advantages of Worklight Studio in the following sections.

Pure native and web development

IBM Worklight Studio provides complete extensibility and compatibility in pure native and web application development. With a very simple wizard, a developer can easily add JavaScript frameworks such as Dojo, jQuery Mobile, and Sencha Touch and IDE provide a WYSIWYG editor for quickly building UIs in a drag-and-drop fashion with the support of UI components.

Shell development and concept

IBM Worklight provides a hybrid shell for mobile applications that offers all capabilities to web and native technologies. By creating a custom shell, you can add third-party native libraries that include Cordova/PhoneGap plugins and can implement custom security modules and extend features specific to enterprise modernization. The shell could be used as enforcement of corporate guideline specifications for designing and security rules. For example, a shell can be utilized to improve and amend default mobile applications or to control native features.

Optimized framework

Worklight Studio provides a common environment to be used as the simple development point that shares all code basis into one stream. An optimization framework consists of the skin concept (runtime skinning) that actually enables an interface for mobile applications depending on the device. This feature enables the runtime interface and enables different sets of customizations. All these settings are device dependent and can easily be transformed to hold any set of code.

Integrated development and mobile simulator

Worklight Studio can be used to develop a component called IBM Worklight Adapters for your application within the same integrated development environment. It allows you to test these adapters thoroughly. It also provides a browser-based mobile simulator for testing web and hybrid applications within IBM Worklight Studio. Mobile simulator is a cross-platform testing module for mobile devices with the support of various Apache Cordova APIs. It allows you to test hybrid applications that use device features without having to run them on the physical device. This reduces redundant development time and effort required for repeated deployment on devices.

Besides this, IBM Worklight Studio allows you to set Ant tasks that can be used to run any mobile application on multiple platforms. IBM Worklight Studio is available in three editions. The Developer edition provides all of the tools needed to build a mobile application. The Consumer edition and Enterprise edition add enterprise-level security and integration with the IBM Application Center.

Worklight Device Runtime

The IBM Worklight Device Runtime component delivers a smooth and uniform bridge between web technologies (HTML5, CSS3, and JavaScript) and the additional native functionalities added to the various platforms. IBM Worklight Device Runtime supports a variety of mobile OS and release levels.

The following screenshot shows the different features in Device Runtime that reduce the complexity and implementation time frame for a developer:

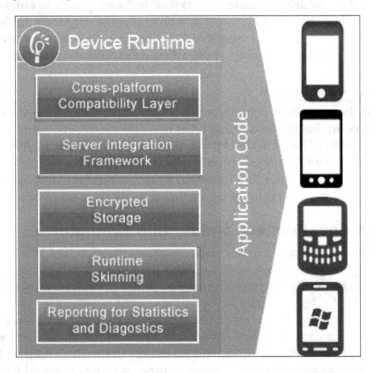

The following section provides details about the various features of Device Runtime:

- **Cross-platform Compatibility Layer**: By using this layer, hybrid mobile applications can access common control elements such as tab bars, clipboards, and native device interface features.

- **Server Integration Framework**: This allows applications to utilize a Server Secure Layer Connection to connect to the server all the time.

- **Encrypted Storage**: This layer helps to access application restoration data in an encryption that helps a user to access data using this API.

- **Reporting for Statistics and Diagnostics**: In this layer, the Mobile application transforms the data and sends it to IBM Worklight Server by executing an event that stores the data in a separate database.

Worklight Server

This component is utilized to bind a client-side/server-side integration with built-in security prevention and helps the application to have a strong communication with the backend system. This complete framework based on the cryptographic module to protect user-specific information as well as server specifications. The following screenshot is of the structure of IBM Worklight Server:

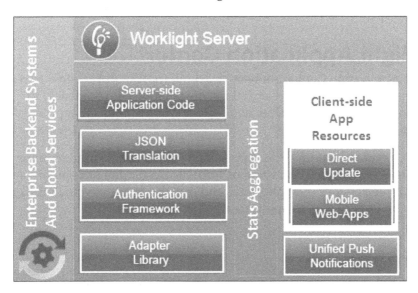

The following is a brief description of the structure of IBM Worklight Server:

- **Server-side Application Code**: This module defends the security and performance of a mobile device. By using this code, you can have direct access to the backend system or cloud-based services.

- **JSON translation**: JSON is a lightweight data structure format, such as XML, that automatically converts hierarchical data responses with optimized consumption.

- **Authentication Framework**: If your mobile application is based on Worklight Server, you can benefit from enterprise-class security, which enables single sign-on using **Lightweight Third Party Authentication (LTPA)**.

Worklight Console

IBM Worklight Console is an administration component based on the web interface. This web-based console is used to enable/disable applications, adapters, and push notification rules.

You can manage a mobile application by activating/deactivating its outdated versions. It can also be used to publish messages or notifications to users regarding new updates and new features released. Worklight Console contains an identifier to ensure security and application provisioning for users. This console also assists administrators with viewing statistics and user information from all running applications on IBM Worklight Server. This helps to make decisions regarding specific platforms, user interaction, and performance overview.

Worklight Application Center

Worklight Application Center is a web-based internal enterprise store to centralize mobile applications, including distribution, installation, and feedback. An application catalog helps to find available mobile applications that provides feedback on application versions.

During the development lifecycle, Application Center can be used to inline the movements of new application versions from the development point of view. It allows multiple versions of applications and can also be utilized to limit versions for any group of users as well as applications.

Summary

In this chapter, we have covered the history and background of IBM Worklight, approaches used in mobile development and why Worklight is the right choice between other mobile application development solutions with its inline efficient tools and components.

In the next chapter, you're going to install Worklight (Worklight Studio and Worklight Server) to set up the development environment on your computer to manage your application's lifecycle from development to deployment. Moreover, you'll be guided in setting up the Android SDK within the same environment to test the application on an Android simulator. This will help you to run and follow along with the examples discussed throughout this book.

2
Installing Worklight

This chapter lists the specific installation and configuration steps to set up the development environment that you need to create in mobile applications with IBM Worklight. It guides you through the steps of installing the software prerequisites and the Eclipse-based IBM Worklight Studio.

In this chapter, we will cover the installation steps for both the IBM Worklight Consumer and Developer Editions with the intention of giving you a complete step-through guide to prepare your development environment for both editions as per your target requirement.

Installing IBM Worklight Consumer Edition

Before starting with the consumer edition installation, we need to have the required software installed in your operating system:

- **Java Runtime Environment (JRE)**
- IBM Installation Manager

To install JRE, please download the setup files from `http://www.oracle.com/technetwork/java/javase/downloads/java-archive-downloads-javase7-521261.html`.

To review the list of supported operating systems and system requirements for IBM Worklight for various versions, please visit `http://www-01.ibm.com/support/docview.wss?uid=swg27024838`.

Installing IBM Installation Manager

IBM Installation Manager is an enterprise deployment tool used to install, modify, and uninstall IBM products. You might already have the Installation Manager installed; if not, you can download this from IBM's website by visiting `http://pic.dhe.ibm.com/infocenter/install/v1r5/index.jsp`.

At this step, assume that you have the IBM Installation Manager installed in your system. Perform the following steps in the Installation Manager after the installation:

1. Now start the IBM Installation Manager to install the IBM product.
2. Navigate to **File | Preferences...** to open the **Preference** window, and use the **Add Repository...** button to add the repository location; you can use physical media or download the product to install it using search services.
3. Click on **OK** to add the repository and return to the main Installation Manager window to start the setup.

 If you're using Windows OS, it is recommended to install the software on root directory like `C:\IBM\Worklight` instead of performing the installation in the `Program Files` folder.

As already covered in *Chapter 1, Getting Started with IBM Worklight*, IBM Worklight Studio is used to implement runtime skins for building apps that automatically suppress the environment, which will be seamlessly deployable using the IBM Worklight Server. IBM Worklight Server provides leverage to its defined resources and infrastructure. Now, we are moving on to the installation of IBM Worklight components with details of their setup files.

To install **IBM Worklight Consumer 5.0.5**, you must have following IBM Worklight Studio, Server, and Eclipse plugin files to step forward:

- `IM_Rep_Worklight_Server_wce_5.0.5.zip`
- `IM_Rep_Worklight_Studio_wce_5.0.5.zip`
- `worklight_studio_wce_5.0.5.zip`

To download Worklight Consumer Edition files, you must have an IBM ID to access and download these files for the desired operating system. Please use the following URL to find the details:

`http://www-01.ibm.com/support/docview.wss?uid=swg24033643`

The listed files are installation sources to set up IBM Worklight Server and Worklight Studio, and the last file is used to set up IBM Worklight Studio plugin which can be installed separately with any Eclipse version.

Installing via an archive file provides several options depending on the operating system and package being installed. The use of the IBM Installation Manager applies to Worklight Studio and Worklight Server packages but is not supported on Mac platforms. The use of the Eclipse update site applies to Worklight Studio that is supported on all platforms. The following sections show you how to install each of the available packages.

Installing IBM Worklight Server

Use the following steps to install the packages:

1. Unzip the listed server archive file into a temporary directory.
2. Start the IBM Installation Manager.
3. Click on **Preferences** in the File menu.
4. Click on **Add Repository**.
5. Enter the fully qualified path to the following directory:

   `unzip-directory/IWS/disk1/`

6. Click on **OK** in the **Add Repository** window.
7. Click on **OK** in the **Preferences** window.
8. Once you return to the main IBM Installation Manager window, click on **Install**.

9. Tick the IBM Worklight Consumer Edition checkbox as shown in the following screenshot:

IBM Installation Manager and installation package selection

10. In the following screenshot, you need to define the installation directory for IBM Worklight and Windows operating system and then click on **Next**.

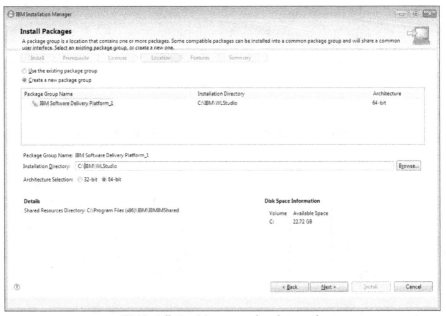

IBM Installation Manager and package path

Configuring a database for the Worklight Server

The installation wizard will now request for a database connection to prepare the different schema for Worklight Server as shown in the following screenshot. In this book, we have used MySQL database, Version 5, for backend. After you have made your selection, click on **Next**.

Database selection for IBM Worklight

Now define the parameters for the database connection, including host, port, and credentials followed by the respective database library (the .jar file). The following screenshot illustrates the required parameters such as database running host, port, and .jar file path to build connection between Worklight Server and Database Server. After you fill it, click on **Next** to move on to the next step:

Database connection parameters

When the connection is successful, as the following screenshot shows, we start with the preparation of three different schemas for Worklight Server.

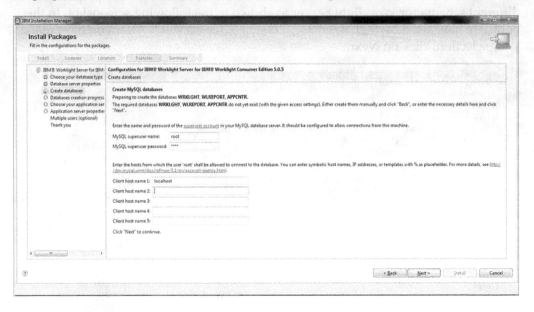

Clicking on the **Next** button will create these schemes in the connected database and show you the status of these SQL queries with their status in the next section.

Configuring WebSphere Application Server (Liberty profile)

We will now configure the WebSphere Application Server. On the server panel, specify the application server on which IBM Worklight will be used. We have chosen the WebSphere Application Server Liberty profile as shown in following screenshot. This means no additional parameters are required, and the application server is created and configured automatically. If this sounds good to you, then click on **Next** to follow the next step.

On the next screen, as seen in the following screenshot, review the directory and server to be selected and finally click on **Install**:

After you are done with the IBM Worklight Server installation, you will see the screen that indicates the installation of WAS (Liberty profile) is complete. Now click on **Finish** to close this window.

It's time to verify the installation of IBM Worklight Server once the installation is complete. We must confirm it by starting the IBM Worklight Server.

For Windows OS, open the command prompt by pressing *Ctrl + R*, type cmd in the **Run** window, and click on **OK**.

Now navigate to the installation directory of IBM Worklight,
`<WorklightInstallDirectory>/server/wlp/bin`, and run the following
command, according to the operating system, under the black screen:

- **Linux:** `sudo ./server start worklightServer`
- **Windows:** `server.bat start worklightServer`

The following screenshot shows the confirmation message you receive when the
Worklight Server starts successfully:

You can also verify whether the IBM Worklight Server started successfully by using
the Worklight console as shown in the following screenshot. The Worklight console
installed with the IBM Worklight Server can be accessed by opening a browser and
navigating to the URL shown in the following screenshot, where `<server_host_`
`name>` is replaced with the hostname on which IBM Worklight Server is installed:

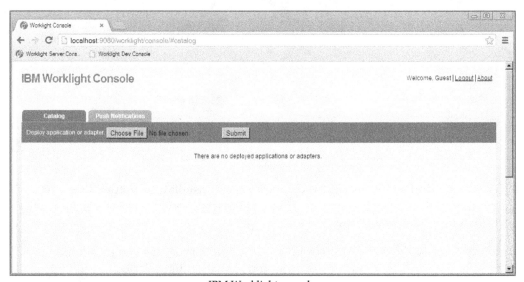

IBM Worklight console

Installing IBM Worklight Studio

To install IBM Worklight Studio, use the IBM installation Manager to add the repository like we did for IBM Worklight Server—just follow the wizard and keep clicking on the next button. Another way to install Eclipse IDE, which is the latest version of Java EE Developer, is to download from `eclipse.org` and install the IBM Worklight Studio plugin in two simple steps:

- Under the heading of archive files, overview of IBM Worklight Studio's repository file is used to install with IBM Installation Manager
- The third file is also the IBM Worklight Studio, but this is a plugin file that can load in the Eclipse IDE

Follow the ensuing steps to install the Worklight Studio plugin in Eclipse IDE:

1. Start the already installed Eclipse (JEE or Classic) Version 4.2.2.
2. Click on **Install New Software** in the **Help** menu.
3. Click on **Add** to open the **Add Repository** window.
4. Click on **Archive** and enter the fully qualified path to the archive file as shown in the following screenshot:

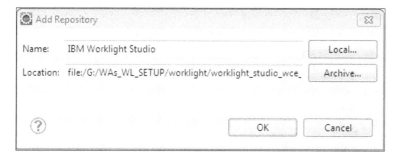

5. Select the items to install as shown in the following screenshot:

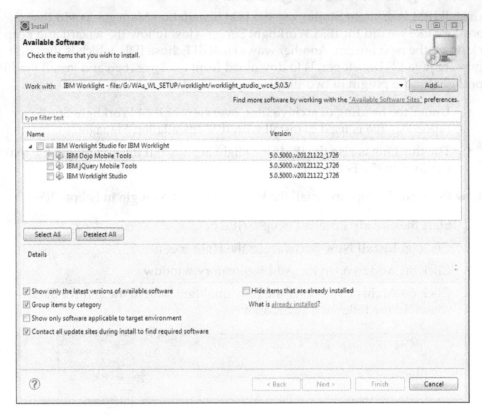

6. Click on **Next** and review the selected tools for installation and accept the license agreement. Click on **Finish** to begin.

7. When the installation is complete, IDE prompts to restart the Eclipse IDE. Click on **Restart**.

IBM Worklight Studio is now installed and ready for use.

Installing IBM Worklight Developer Edition

If you are using Eclipse in IDE and need to use the IBM Worklight Developer Edition, use the following steps:

1. Install Eclipse Juno 4.2.2 or Eclipse IDE for Java EE Developers.

2. Download the .zip file from the given URL and make sure that file name is iws_update_site_wde.5.0.6.2.zip as we are targeting IBM Worklight v5: http://public.dhe.ibm.com/ibmdl/export/pub/software/mobile-solutions/worklight/

3. Start Eclipse and then navigate to **Help | Install New Software**...

4. Click on **Add** to open the **Add Repository** window.

5. Click on **Archive** and enter the fully qualified path to the archive file you just downloaded using the preceding URL.

6. Select **IBM Worklight Studio Development Tools** and click on **Next**.

7. On the **Install Details** page, select the features of Worklight Studio that you want to install and then click on **Next**.

8. You should always select **IBM Worklight Studio**. The **IBM Dojo Mobile Tools** and **IBM jQuery Mobile Tools** are optional; select them based on your anticipated use.

9. Click on **Next**, review and accept the license terms, and then click on **Finish** to begin with the installation.

10. Follow the prompts to complete the installation.

Installing Android SDK

Android proposes a custom plugin for the Eclipse IDE named **Android Development Tools** (**ADT**). It accelerates the capabilities of Eclipse and quickly provides you with the option to start up a new Android project, including a simulator. The ADT plugin for Eclipse is an integrated environment in which you can build, debug, and test Android-native applications. The Android SDK provides the tools and APIs that are required to develop an application on the Android platform by using Java programming language.

The initial step is to download the Android SDK, which is not present with IBM Worklight Studio and must be downloaded from `http://developer.android.com/sdk/index.html`.

Decompress the downloaded Android SDK file and copy the folder to the location where you store SDKs or other development-related files.

To install the Android Development Tools (ADT) plugin for Eclipse, use the following steps:

1. Start Eclipse and navigate to **Help | Install New Software**. This opens the **Available Software** window.

2. To add, download, and install the ADT plugin, click on **Add** to open the **Add Repository** dialog. Please enter the name ADT Plugin in the **Name** field and the plugin's location https://dl-ssl.google.com/android/eclipse/ in the **Location** field, as shown in the following screenshot:

3. Then click on **OK**. The button will start loading and then it shows the ADT plugin features available to install from the **Available Software** window. Check the **Developer Tools** checkbox and click on **Next**.

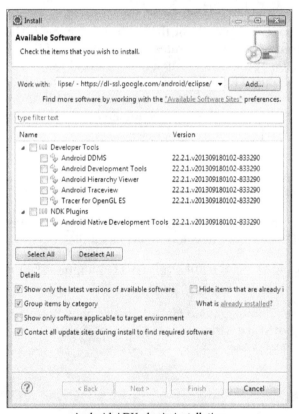

Android ADK plugin installation

4. Complete the installation wizard and accept the default settings.

5. You must restart Eclipse in order to make the changes work.

6. After Eclipse is restarted, if it prompts a warning for an Android SDK, click on **Open Preferences** on the warning message dialog to open the preference window. Select **Android** from the left panel, and now on the right panel, click on the **Browse SDK Location** path and select the android SDK folder. Click on **OK** to resolve this warning.

7. In the **Android SDK Manager** window (see the following screenshot), select **Android SDK Platform-tools** and **Android Support Library**, and select specific Android versions to test your application.

8. Once you've finished selecting what you require, click on **Install**. This will start the installation process in a few steps. Once the installation completes, click on the close icon to close the **Android SDK Manager** window.

To configure an Android virtual device, use the following steps:

1. Within Eclipse, navigate to **Window | Android Virtual Device Manager** from the menu.

2. Clicking on **New** will open a dialog where you create a new Android Virtual Device (AVD). Give the AVD a name, such as GNexusAVD, as shown in following screenshot:

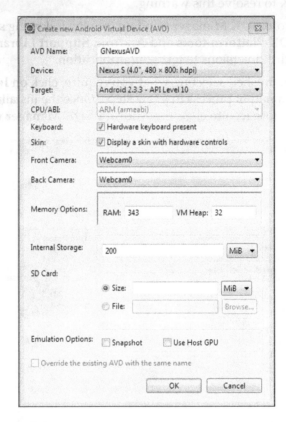

The new Android Virtual Device is now ready for use to test and run the application. If additional devices are needed, repeat the preceding steps.

Summary

In this chapter, we have covered the installation of IBM Worklight Server and IBM Worklight Studio with the help of the IBM Installation Manager to set up the development environment. We also covered the installation of the IBM Worklight Studio along with a plugin for Eclipse in case you want to use Eclipse for Worklight app development in your machine. We also covered the installation of the IBM Worklight Development Edition to start Worklight development with no cost. In the next chapter, we are going to create our first Worklight application using the same setup environment and cover other IBM Worklight components that we had discussed in the first chapter.

3

Creating a Basic Worklight Application

In this chapter, we will learn how to build a simple "Hello World" application for different environments, gain an understanding of the project directory structure, and learn how to create skins for specific devices. Using Worklight to create user interfaces offers a big development advantage on the client and server sides. In general, developers face problems during development. Support for the creation of hybrid apps using other products is typically not easy to define use cases and conduct debugging and preview testing for enterprise applications. However, with Worklight, developers can create simple architecture and amend enhanced structures to generate mobile application.

Creating a simple IBM Worklight application

Let's start by creating a simple HelloWorld Worklight project.

 The steps described for creating an app are similar for IBM Worklight Studio and Eclipse IDE.

The following is what you'll need to do:

1. Start IBM Worklight Studio.

2. Navigate to **File** | **New** and select **Worklight Project**, as shown in the following screenshot:

Creating a new Worklight project

3. In the dialog that is displayed in the following screenshot, select **Hybrid Application** as the type of application defined in project templates, enter `HelloWorld` as the name of the first mobile project, and click on **Next**.

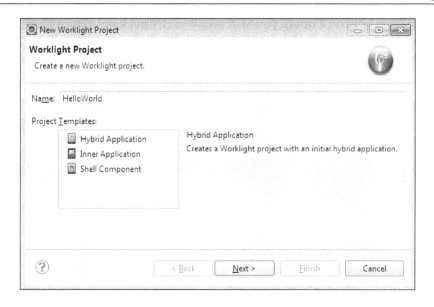

4. You will see another dialog for **Hybrid Application**. In **Application name**, provide `HelloWorld` as the name of the application. Leave the checkboxes unchecked for now; these are used to extend supported JavaScript libraries into the app. Click on **Finish**.

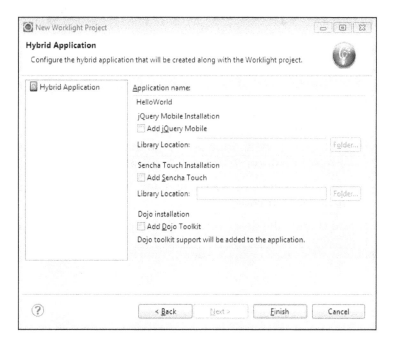

5. After clicking on **Finish**, you will see your project has been created from design perspective in **Project Explorer**, as shown in the following screenshot:

Worklight project and application structure

The project name used within Worklight Studio is HelloWorld, and the display name of the app will be HelloWorld, as defined earlier in step 4 of the *Creating a simple IBM Worklight application* section. To change the name, follow the steps defined as follows:

1. If the project is not opened, double-click on the application-descriptor. xml file in **Project Explorer** to open in Application Descriptor Editor.

2. On the design tab, change the **Display name** attribute from HelloWorld to any other name of your choice.

    You can also change the description by editing the **Description** attribute.

3. Save and close the application-descriptor.xml file.

Now, let's move on to the structure of the application. The default environment is called the common environment. It is responsible for holding every component and file related to the app, which shares its resources with the environment.

Application resources

In order to run the Worklight app on multiple devices, you must have the following resource files in your project. IBM Worklight automatically generates any missing resources that are not supplied. These resources are inter-related with each other.

- `HelloWorld.html`: This is the main HTML file that acts as the interface of the mobile application. This file loads all the web resources (script and style sheets) necessary to define the general components of the application and to hook required document events. By default, this file is placed under the `common` folder.

- `css`: This folder extends or overrides both common files to keep the structure in the framework. It consists of the following files:

    ○ `HelloWorld.css`: This is the main CSS file

    ○ `Reset.css`: This file brings all rendering-oriented engines to a common ground

- `images`: This folder contains images for separate image locations to be called in HTML, directly or using CSS.

- `js`: This folder extends the application instance object and common app class. It contains some predefined files:

    ○ `HelloWorld.js`: This is the main application JavaScript file.

    ○ `Message.js`: This JavaScript file holds JSON objects that contain app messages. It can be used as a source for localization translation.

- `application-descriptor.xml`: This file holds application metadata. Its attributes will be discussed during deployment of this application later in this chapter.

In the following screenshot, we highlight the project application structure and resources:

The common directory structure of a Worklight app

If you proceed with the hybrid application wizard you will have server-side configuration under the following folders structure:

- `bin`: This folder contains generated `.wlapp` and `.wladapter` files that can be used to deploy to a remote Worklight server.

- `server`: This folder is used for server-side customization of a project.

  - `Conf`: This folder contains a file called `worklight.properties`, used to set up properties for the server

  - `authenticationConfig.xml`: This file is used to set authentication realms

  - `login.html`: This file is used to present a login form for web environments and Worklight Console

- `java`: This folder holds Java classes that will be compiled and deployed to IBM Worklight Server for handling customized Java code-based application.

- `lib`: This folder contains some additional JAR files that can be used to extend Java class functionalities and can be deployed on the server. You can see the folder structure of the `bin` and `server` folders in the following screenshot:

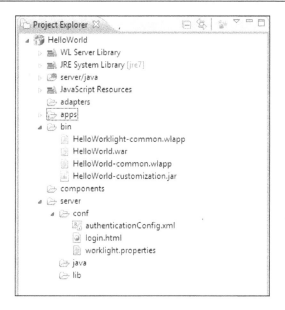

Now put in some additional code to provide a better display to your mobile application:

1. Open `HelloWorld/common/css/HelloWorld.css` and add the following lines to define style:

```css
/* HelloWorld CSS */
#AppBody {
  height: 460px;
  margin: 0 auto;
  width: 320px;
  background-color: #ccc;
  overflow: hidden;
  overflow-y: auto;
}
#header {
  text-align: center;
  background-color: #1D4D90;
  color: #F9FAFB;
  font-size: 16px;
  height: 38px;
  line-height: 38px;
  border-bottom: 1px solid #BBBBBB;
}
#wrapper {
  padding: 10px;
}
```

Downloading the example code

You can download the example code files for all Packt books you have purchased through your account at http://www.packtpub.com. If you purchased this book elsewhere, you can visit http://www.packtpub.com/support and register to have the files e-mailed directly to you.

2. Now move to the main HTML file named HelloWorld.html in the app/common folder. When you open this file, you'll find generated code with referenced script and CSS files within the same with <body> tag.

   Note that the <body> tag must have the ID attribute value set to the content. If you change the value, the application environment does not initialize correctly.

3. Now place the following lines of the code under the <body> tag:

```
<div id="AppBody">
  <div id="header">
  <div id="wrapper"> Welcome </div>
  </div>
  Hello World
</div>
```

Now our HelloWorld application is done. You can preview our first designed page in **Rich Page Editor (RPE)** provided by IDE.

Rich Page Editor

The Rich Page Editor provides an interface for the development of mobile applications. This interface comprises easily editable HTML files and can be added to the Dojo and jQuery widgets. It is commonly used for multitabbed editors, which show multiple page views of different representations of an HTML page. There are three components—Source, Design, and Split views—in Rich Page Editor with which you can view and work with your files or page.

Every view in Rich Page Editor works in conjunction with several other tools that can be used to show in the web page previews. The source view component helps you to view its interface with the source code directly. Besides this, the view contains Mobile, Palette, Outline, and Properties views as a source for user interface.

Split view shows both the interface and the source code on the same page to help you visualize your changes as you make them. You can split the view horizontally or vertically. The following screenshot shows our first designed page in Split view:

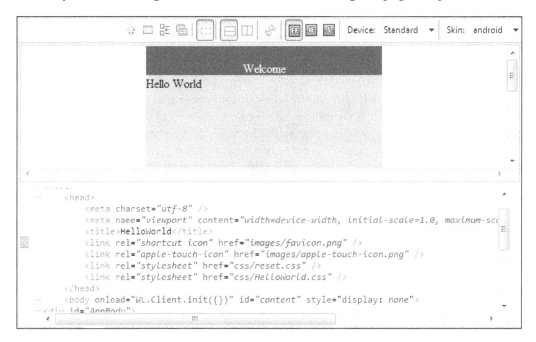

Design view provides the functionality of a WYSIWYG environment. It helps to create and edit files while you're viewing your source code and the actual interface reflects every single change. It provides complete visual interaction to the developer with its feature that allows dragging-and-dropping items and components from palettes and enterprise explorer views. These tabular enhancements have features for device selection as well, which provides a holistic view for device specification and skins you created for every environment. This preview holds compatibilities as browser, so if anyone needs to testify any mobile web application then it can be highly recommended for it. Whereas, device selects the size of any specified mobile to view and to have the effects related to size. Skin selection allows you to use your defined view for Android, iPhone, or Blackberry. By selecting the particular skin, you can switch to another device-specific style view to modify the layout and appearance of the page.

Once we are done with verifying the page layout and text in RPE, it is ready to test on different mobile platforms by using the *Adding Environment* feature of IBM Worklight Studio.

Adding an environment

We have covered IBM Worklight Studio features and what they offer developers. It's time to see how this tool and plugin will make your life even easier. The cross-platform development feature is a great deal to implement. It provides you with the means to achieve cross-development environment without any hurdles and with just a few clicks within its efficient interface. In *Chapter 5, Adding an Adapter*, we will cover this topic in detail for other environments as well.

To add an environment for Android, iPhone, or any other platform, right-click on the Apps folder next to the adapters and navigate to **New | Worklight Environment**. You will see that a dialog box appears with checkboxes for currently supported environments, which you need to create an application for. The following screenshot illustrates this feature—we're adding an Android environment for this application:

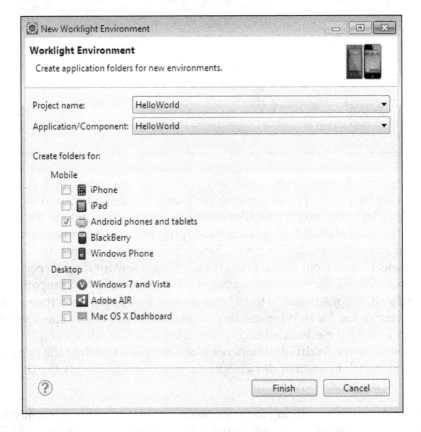

After clicking on the **Finish** button, Studio automatically transforms and generates an Android project for you. In the following screenshot, you can see the android icon, which contains native directories for its source code:

The following tasks should be completed to build the mobile application for any specific environment:

- Verifying the server configuration
- Building the application

Verifying the server configuration

You will use the local development server provided by IBM Worklight Studio. Before we start the bringing together of application components, you should verify the ports and server URL defined in `application-descriptor.xml` under the `<WorklightServerRootURL>` tag. Please use the following steps to configure your application for server communication:

1. Open the file named `application-descriptor.xml` within the `app/HelloWorld` folder.

2. Locate the tag `<worklightServerRootURL>`.

3. Adjust your Worklight server name and port to match the target environment using the following format:

```
<worklightServerRootURL>
  http://[wl_server_name][:port][/path]
</worklightServerRootURL>
```

4. Save and close the `application-descriptor.xml` file.

Please look at the following screenshot for the preceding changes in `application-descriptor.xml`:

```
application-descriptor.xml
    <?xml version="1.0" encoding="UTF-8"?>

            <!-- Licensed Materials - Property of IBM
                5725-G92 (C) Copyright IBM Corp. 2006, 2012. All Rights Reserved.
                US Government Users Restricted Rights - Use, duplication or
                disclosure restricted by GSA ADP Schedule Contract with IBM Corp. -->

    <!-- Attribute "id" must be identical to application folder name -->
    <application id="HelloWorld" platformVersion="5.0"
        xmlns="http://www.worklight.com/application-descriptor"
        xmlns:xsi="http://www.w3.org/2001/XMLSchema-instance">

        <displayName>HelloWorld</displayName>
        <description>HelloWorld</description>
        <author>
            <name>application's author</name>
            <email>application author's e-mail</email>
            <copyright>Copyright My Company</copyright>
            <homepage>http://mycompany.com</homepage>
        </author>
        <height>460</height>
        <width>320</width>
        <mainFile>HelloWorld.html</mainFile>
        <thumbnailImage>common/images/thumbnail.png</thumbnailImage>
        <usage requireAuthentication="never" />
        <worklightServerRootURL>http://${local.IPAddress}:8080</worklightServerRootURL>

    </application>
```

Building the application

The specified project web application archive and Worklight application files must be deployed to IBM Worklight Server for every specified environment. The following are the files that must be built and generated to deploy and run the HelloWorld application on Worklight Server:

- `HelloWorld.war`
- `HelloWorld.wlapp`
- `HelloWorld-android.wlapp` (for Android)

These `.wlapp` files contain the actual web content of the application, which includes the HTML, CSS, and JavaScript files that were created in the previous section.

Application skins

If you need to create a piece of code that determines a specific device, you have to create a separate skin.

To set up the application skin, right-click on **Worklight Application** in **New Worklight Application Skin**. In the dialog box that appears, select the environment for which you need to create a skin for the mobile application.

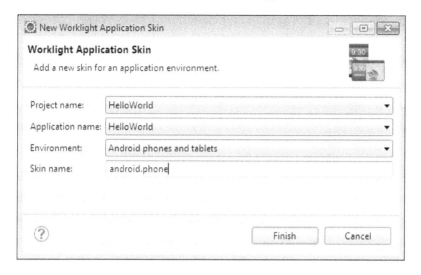

This folder describes the Android skin, which contains HTML, CSS, and JS. The skin for every defined environment is situated within the apps folder shown in the following screenshot. This folder will be responsible for selecting the screen to be loaded in the specified environment.

Skins are a sub variant that tells the related family of style classes to choose the identified skin as the interface of that specified environment. At runtime, only the skin that corresponds to the target device is applied.

 Application skins are supported only for these environments: Android, iPhone, iPad, and BlackBerry 6, 7, and 10.

Previewing an application in the mobile simulator

The last step to executing the application is to deploy it on Worklight Server. Use the following steps to achieve that:

1. Select the HelloWorld project, right-click on app/HelloWorld/common, and navigate to **Run As | Build All and Deploy**.

2. Open the browser and provide the URL http://<wl_server_name>:[port]/console.

3. You will see Worklight Console, where you can see the deployed applications and adapters. The following screenshot shows the console web interface:

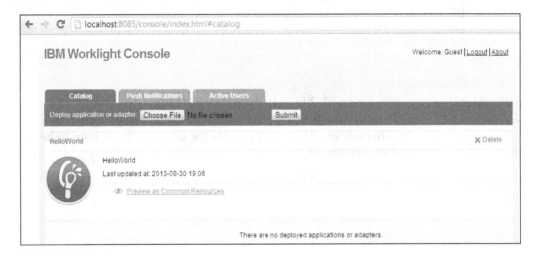

To preview your developed application in Android, perform the following steps:

1. Right-click on **Project App** and navigate to **Run As | Build All and Deploy**.

2. You will see an Android project created with the name **HelloWorldHelloWorldAndroid**. This is the Android project that is generated on behalf of your Worklight app.

3. Right-click on **Android Project** and then navigate to **Run As | Android Application**. You will see the simulator is running and loading your application as shown in the following screenshot:

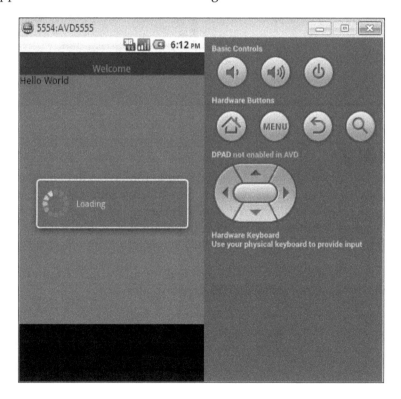

4. After loading is complete, you will see your Worklight hybrid mobile application is running on Android.

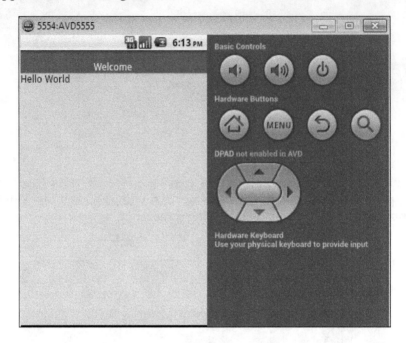

Summary

In this chapter, we covered steps to create a simple IBM Worklight application in the Android environment and an overview of resources. Skin environments are also highlighted with respect to different mobile interfaces. We talked about Rich Page Editor, environment settings, and server configuration, which will allow you to proceed with mobile development using IBM Worklight in an efficient way.

We will be looking at some frameworks and features in the next chapter that will provide more core development expertise to the reader.

4
Customizing the Worklight Application

Hybrid mobile applications are certainly reliable and have consistently proven to be efficient for the implementation of scenarios. These applications can access native mobile features such as the camera, compass, directories, and settings. This reduces costs and the duration of the development life cycle, which is the biggest advantage. In this chapter, we will have an introduction to and learn how to develop mobile applications with IBM Worklight.

If your perspective is primarily relevant to marketing or public interaction, a hybrid application is almost always going to make sense as a practical first step in your mobile outreach strategy. This is because a hybrid application has a number of advantages over native applications, including broader accessibility, compatibility, and cost-effectiveness. We will now discuss web technologies in detail.

A quick overview of HTML5

HTML5 is the most versatile and easy-to-use web technology in the modern world. Most of it has been constructed in **Web Hypertext Application Technology Working Group** (**WHATWG**). The World Wide Web's markup language has always been HTML. HTML was mainly created to make web development an easy task. Besides, the general design and adaptations have made it possible to utilize HTML to define a number of documents. The area of concern that's been occasionally addressed by HTML is ambiguous and is referred to as Web Application Development. This HTML specification attempts to improve web application development structure. In this specification, the ability to update HTML references in order to address issues regarding web compatibility has also been enhanced.

The IBM Worklight client-side API

In this chapter, you will learn how the IBM Worklight client-side API can improve mobile application development. You will also see the IBM Worklight server-side API improve client/server integration and communication between mobile applications and back end systems.

The IBM Worklight client-side API allows mobile applications to access most of the features that are available in IBM Worklight during runtime, in order to get access to some defined libraries that appear to be bundled into the mobile application. Integration of the libraries for your mobile application using Worklight Server is used to access predefined communication interfaces. These libraries also offer unified access to native device features, which streamlines application development.

The IBM Worklight client-side API contains hybrid, native, mixed hybrid, and web-based APIs. Besides, it extends those of these APIs that are responsible for supporting every mobile development framework. The development framework for a mobile application is used to improve security including custom and built-in authentication mechanisms for IBM Worklight provided by client-side API modules. It provides a semantic connection between web technologies such as HTML5, CSS3, and JavaScript with native functions that are available for different mobile platforms.

The WLClient JavaScript client library

This collection of topics lists the public methods of the IBM Worklight runtime client API for mobile apps, desktop, and the Web.

WLClient is a JavaScript client library that provides access to IBM Worklight capabilities. This library initializes the re-rendering of applications. It manages the authenticated sessions, all general information handling, data corporate information systems for the purpose of manipulation, storing and retrieving user preferences throughout the sessions, internationalized application texts, and environment-specific UI behavior. It stores the custom log lines, which deal with special tables that exist in the database, in order to prepare audits and reports. It is used to write debug lines on the logger window and device-specific functions for iPhone, Android, Windows Mobile, and BlackBerry.

It contains asynchronous JavaScript calls, which takes an `options` parameter. In reply to the JavaScript call, success and failure handlers receive a response parameter. The API consists of many non-linear calls, which we will be demonstrating here.

The function `onSuccess` is used to initialize the application. If an `onFailure` function is not passed, a default `onFailure` function is called. If `onFailure` is passed, it overrides any specific failure-handling function. The `WL.Client` library contains the following methods:

- `WL.Client.init`: This method sets the `WL.Client` object. The options for methods are present in the `initOptions.js` file. The syntax for `WL.Client. init` is `WL.Client.init({options})`.

- `WL.Client.invokeProcedure`: This is a method that invokes a procedure that is exposed by an IBM Worklight Adapter. The syntax for `WL.Client. invokeProcedure` is `WL.Client invokeProcedure (invocationData, options)`.

- `WL.Client.isConnected`: This is a method that has been deprecated since IBM Worklight v4.1.3. Use the `WL.Device.getNetworkInfo` method instead. It returns `true` if the application is connected to IBM Worklight Server. The syntax for `WL.Client.isConnected` is: `WL.Client.isConnected()`.

- `WL.Client.isUserAuthenticated`: This is a method that checks whether the user is authenticated in a specified resource realm or in the resource realm that was assigned to the application when it was deployed. This method returns `true` if the user is authenticated in the realm and `false` otherwise. The syntax for `WL.Client.isUserAuthenticated` is `WL.Client. isUserAuthenticated(realm)`.

- `WL.Client.login`: This method is used to log in to a specific realm and it is an asynchronous function. The syntax for `WL.Client.login` is `WL.Client. login(realm, options)`.

- `WL.Client.logout`: This method logs out to a specific realm and it is an asynchronous function. The syntax for `WL.Client.logout` is `WL.Client. logout(realm, options)`.

Besides these, there are some other `WL.Client` implementations that are stated according to the behavior of a particular application.

Exploring Dojo Mobile

Regarding the Dojo UI framework, you'll learn about Dojo Mobile in detail. Dojo Mobile, an extension for Dojo Toolkit, provides a series of widgets, or components, optimized for use on a mobile device, such as a smartphone or tablet. The Dojo framework is an extension of JavaScript and provides a built-in library which contains custom components such as text fields, validation menus, and image galleries. The components are modelled on their native counterparts and will look and feel native to those familiar with smartphone applications. The components are completely customizable using themes that let you make various customizations, such as pushing different sets of styles to iOS and Android users.

Designing your first Dojo application

In this section, you will learn how to build a very simple mobile application that contains some basic Dojo components in only a few steps using Worklight Studio. You will also learn how to use the Dojo Mobile Application architecture with page views, listItems, and Dojo Toolkit implementation. It is a JavaScript framework that enables cross-platform development of mobile applications.

The following steps show you how to create a mobile application, using the browser visualization, Worklight Studio virtualization.

1. To start with, create a Worklight hybrid application.

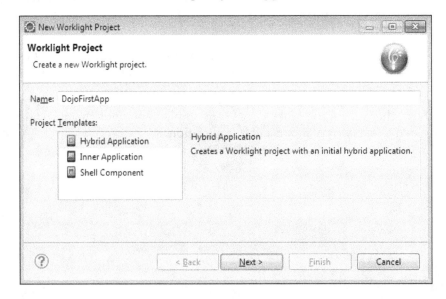

2. Select the checkbox to add Dojo Toolkit. It will automatically add Dojo Toolkit to the environment of the particular application.

3. Click on **Finish**.

4. The following screenshot shows the folder structure of the project `DojoFirstApp`, which includes complete Dojo Toolkit.

5. After the completion of the **New Worklight Project** wizard, look at the right-hand side of Worklight Studio. A palette view appears, in which you will find Dojo widgets and components. You can choose any of the widgets for your application. The following screenshot shows the Dojo palette:

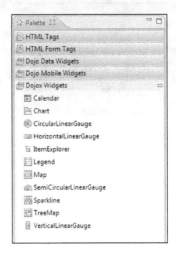

6. Open `apps/HelloWorld/common/HelloWorld.html`. Select its **Design** view instead of **Source** or **Split**.

7. Select **View**, under **Dojo Mobile Widgets** and drag it to the **Design** screen of your HTML page named `HelloWorld.html`. Define the parameters as shown in the following screenshot and then hit **Finish**:

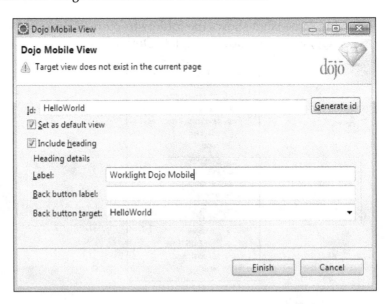

8. You will see the **Design** view as shown in the following screenshot:

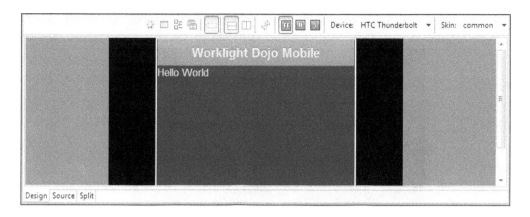

9. If you click on the **Source** or **Split** options, you'll have the following code to generate a mobile screen with a header:

```
<div data-dojo-type="dojox.mobile.View" id="HelloWorld"
  data-dojo-props="selected:true">
<h1 data-dojo-type="dojox.mobile.Heading"
    data-dojo-props="label:'Worklight Dojo
Mobile',moveTo:'HelloWorld'"></h1>
</div>
```

10. Click on **ListItem** and drag it to the page view.

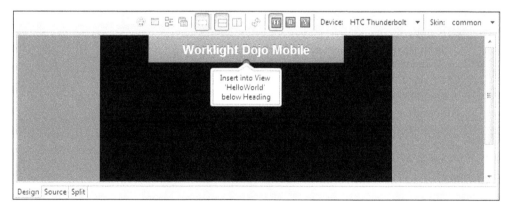

11. These are actually list items so provide the data in sequence. The following screenshot shows a basic view of list items, you can add as many as you need.

The following is the complete code after adding the header and **ListItem** into our mobile application:

```
<body onload="WL.Client.init({})" id="content" style="display: none">
  <div data-dojo-type="dojox.mobile.View" id="HelloWorld"
    data-dojo-props="selected:true">
    <h1 data-dojo-type="dojox.mobile.Heading"
      data-dojo-props="label:'Worklight Dojo
Mobile',moveTo:'HelloWorld'"></h1>
    <div data-dojo-type="dojox.mobile.ListItem"
      data-dojo-props="label:'ListItem3'"></div>
    <div data-dojo-type="dojox.mobile.ListItem"
      data-dojo-props="label:'ListItem2'"></div>
    <div data-dojo-type="dojox.mobile.ListItem"
      data-dojo-props="label:'ListItem3'"></div>
  </div>
  <!-- application UI goes here -->
  <script src="js/HelloWorld.js"></script>
  <script src="js/messages.js"></script>
  <script src="js/auth.js"></script>
</body>
```

Adding an environment in IBM Worklight

Using Worklight Studio, developers can simply add environments to their Worklight application and start writing code that is specific to multiple mobile or web environments. If you need to maintain a version of your IBM Worklight application for any specific mobile platform, then you should add the environment that originated from a particular platform to your application. For instance, if you want to create an Android version of your Worklight app, you must add an Android environment. When you start adding an environment in your application, it actually creates a new folder, called the common folder, for that specified environment. It contains all the resources for that new environment.

While creating a project in Worklight, it creates a common folder within the app to use web technologies such as HTML5 and JS to implement UI and logic with frameworks such as jQuery and Dojo. This common folder stores its files in the following structure:

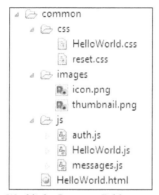

The Worklight Common Folder structure

If we move on this folder hierarchy, the images folder holds images; these images override existing images with the same names in the common environment. The css folder holds styling files that override or extend the CSS and stylesheet files in the common environment, while the js folder holds JavaScript files that override the common JavaScript objects within the application. The class that is defined in the desired environment folder overrides the common app class. Finally, the new HTML file extends the prebuilt HTML file in common Worklight environment that has a similar name.

The common folder in the Worklight application is responsible for holding the code you write to design or develop pages. Other resources are transferred from this folder to several environments.

Let's start with adding the Android environment to our Dojo sample app, which we created in the previous chapter. Please perform the following steps:

1. Open your application in Worklight Studio or Eclipse. To learn how to create a Worklight project, please have a look at the previous chapter. The following screenshot shows the structure of a Worklight application in **Project Explorer**:

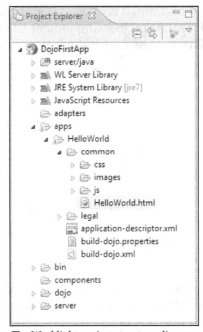

The Worklight project structure diagram

2. To add the Android environment into your Worklight application, right-click on the project and follow the menu as shown in following screenshot, and navigate to **New | Worklight Environment**.

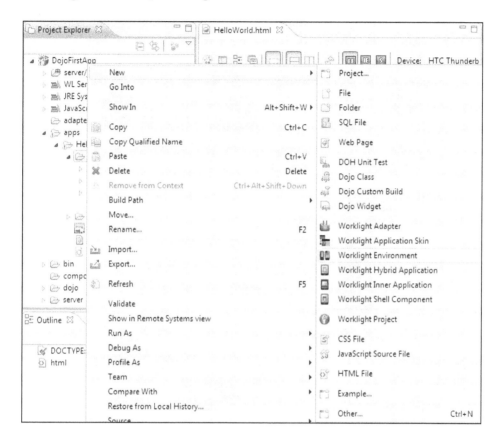

3. It will open the **Worklight Environment** window, where you need to fill up the required values for adding an environment in your project. Include the **Project name** combobox for the selection of a Worklight project and the **Application/Component** combobox to select a Worklight application. Finally, select the Android environment checkbox between other environment checkboxes as shown in the following screenshot:

Adding a mobile/desktop Worklight environment

4. Click on the **Finish** button.

After completion of all the preceding steps, you can see the `android` folder structure as shown in the following screenshot:

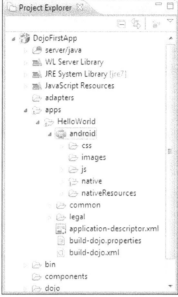

The Android environment

Now, we can move on with a brief description regarding specific environment resources.

Application resources

The Worklight platform allows developers to write applications by means of web or native technologies. Both technologies can also be used in a single app. Both web and native client-side app resources must be placed under the `common` folder with a predefined structure. Depending on the environment selection, IBM Worklight Studio uses the `application` folder to generate and build these resources into the `app` folder. However, to maintain production quality, you should provide all defined resources that are mandatory for those environments in which the application is executed.

Application-descriptor

The descriptor file contains metadata that is used to declare and define various facets of the native API for the Android application.

This application-descriptor is written and can be modified in XML and a mandatory file that allows you to store metadata in the root directory of the application. This application descriptor file is automatically generated by Worklight Studio when you initiate or create a Worklight application. In addition, this file can be improvised to add some custom properties.

This metadata file handles property identifications, which will be used to declare various attributes of the application. Worklight provides this file, named `application-descriptor.xml`, located in the application's root directory.

The following code example shows the format of the the `application-descriptor.xml` file for native API applications for Android:

```
<?xml version="1.0" encoding="UTF-8"?>
<nativeAndroidApp
    id="android"
    platformVersion="5.0.5"
    securityTest="security test name"
    version="1.0"
    xmlns="http://www.worklight.com/native-android-descriptor">
    <displayName>HelloWorld</displayName>
    <description>HelloWorld</description>
    <publicSigningKey>application public signing key</
publicSigningKey>
</nativeAndroidApp>
```

Let's understand line by line what it means to the application. To start with, the `<nativeAndroidApp>` tag is actually used to define the Android environment or added automatically when the developer adds the Android environment to the application. This is the key element as you can see it contains multiple attributes to configure the Android environment within the Worklight application. It has three mandatory attributes, while one is optional as follows:

- `id`: This attribute defines the unique identification of the application. The ID should be unique to the name of the application folder. It must be a string that holds an alphanumeric character that must start with a letter. It may have an underscore '_' character.

- `platformVersion`: This contains the platform version of IBM Worklight that is used to build or develop the application.

- `version`: This element is used to assign the version of the application. This value of the `version` attribute is a string that contains the major and minor version numbers of the application. It is highlighted and visible on the Marketplace or App Store, wherever the application is deployed for users to download.

- `securityTest`: This attribute is optional but it is subjected to specify a security configuration. In case you give the client access to a protected resource, this security implementation checks the client authentication. In case of failure, Worklight initiates the process to authenticate based on the credentials passed on.

The main HTML file

At the time of creating a Worklight application, one HTML file is constructed by IBM Studio. We name the HTML file with the name of your app and use it to control and design the UI of the application. This file is responsible for loading all the resources that contain JavaScript and CSS. We need these to define the common elements of the application, in which a script file is used to obtain the document events.

This main HTML file is located in the `app/common` directory and must contain a `body` tag, and to set as content you must have the `Id` attribute defined in the `body` tag. If the value is changed, the environment of the application is not initialized correctly.

Client scripts and stylesheets

JavaScript files are used to implement business logic and query integration between the backend and predefined structures such as challenge handlers and message dictionaries. These structures automatically translate the defined string according to the declared values in a designated file. All the scripts files are placed under the `app/common/js` folder. CSS files are used to style application views and are placed under the `common/css` folder.

The application icon

The application icon is used to specify the graphical identification of the created app. The Worklight application comes with the default thumbnail image on creating the app. Replacing the icon image would override the default image. This image must be square and preferably of pixel 128 x 128 in size and placed under the `common/images` folder of the app.

The splash screen

IBM Worklight creates the default splash image for each application environment when adding the environment to the app. The splash screen loads with the image while the application is being initialized. As it applies only to mobile environments, the developer can change the default image by overriding it; the image dimension must be the same as that of the app. This splash image can be found under the `[Environment]/native/www` folder.

The Worklight client property file

When adding an environment in the IBM Worklight application, Studio will create the required native API and the client property file for the corresponding environment in the Worklight project. The name and the content format are dependent on the selected environment.

Please follow this table for details in sequence:

Environment	Worklight native and client properties
iOS	The `WorklightAPI` folder defines the IBM Worklight native library. The `worklight.plist` file is the client property file.
Android	The `worklight-android.jar` file defines the IBM Worklight native library. The `wlclient.properties` file is the client property file.
Java ME	The `worklight-javame.jar` file and the `json4javame.jar` file together define the IBM Worklight native library. The `wlclient.properties` file is the client property file.

These are brief descriptions to determine the property files with respect to the environment.

The following screenshot shows you the Android resource hierarchy generated by deploying the app to the Android environment.

You must define the properties of this client property file before using it in your native app for Android.

The following table lists the properties of the `wlclient.properties` file, their descriptions, and possible examples for their values:

Property	Description	Values
wlServerProtocol	This is the communication protocol for the Worklight Server.	Http or https
wlServerHost	This is the host name of the Worklight Server.	localhost or HostIP
wlServerPort	This is the port for the IBM Worklight Server. If this value is left blank, the default port is used. If the value of the wlServerProtocol property is https, you must leave this value blank.	8080 or defined
wlServerContext	This is the server context, which is automatically generated.	/
wlAppId	This is the application ID, as defined in the application-descriptor.xml file.	HelloWorld or AppName
wlAppVersion	This is the application version, as defined in the application-descriptor.xml file.	1.0
wlEnvironment	This property defines the IBM Worklight environment. You must not modify the value of this property.	androidnative

Exploring the Android application environment

The Android environment for Worklight apps provides complete implementation and structured resource handling for handling the environment. Here, we have to generate the Android native project by deploying the Android environment added to the Worklight project/app. Follow the given steps to initialize the Android project for a particular environment:

1. Right-click on **apps** and navigate to **HelloWorld | android**.

2. On the menu that appears, select **Run As | 2 Build Environment and Deploy**. After clicking on this option, the deployment process will start and the status can be seen in the **Console** window under **Worklight Studio | Eclipse**.

3. After deployment of the environment, you can see the Android project generated in the same workspace with a combination of project name, app name, and selected mobile/desktop environment.

An Android project generated after build

The the Android application is finally generated and ready to execute with the resources. Now, we will brief you about the Android native project resource structure. You will see a basic Android application. The following table describes the structure and information of each folder that every Android project contains:

Folder	Description
src	This folder holds the Java files.
gen	Once the project is compiled with no error, this folder holds the generated Java files by Android Development Toolkit. It also includes R.java and interfaces created from the **Android Interface Definition Language** (**AIDL**) files.
res	This folder is used to store application resource files, including drawable files such as images, application activities layout files, and string values.
res/drawable	The drawable folder is used to store the several bitmap files such as PNG, JPEG, GIF, and 9-patch image files and a list of drawable resources supported by the Android OS.
res/values	The values folder holds XML files that are used to store various strings specifying name and variable relationships. These strings are generated by reference in the R class for them to be accessed anywhere in the project.
res/layout	The layout folder holds the layout files. They are written in XML and are used to define and organize Android objects (for example, textboxes, buttons, and so on) on the screen with different layouts supported in the Android OS.

Android also has some major files in the project. Let start exploring them one by one:

- AndroidManifest.xml: This XML file is one of the core files of the Android project. It holds overall information about application services and activities and is used to define permissions for applications such as allowing an application to access the Internet or allowing an application to write.

- MainLayout.xml: This file describes the layout of the page. This means it is responsible for the placement of every component (such as textboxes, labels, radio buttons, user defined components, and so on) on the app screen.

- Activity: Every application that occupies the entire device screen needs at least one class that inherits from the Activity class. One major method is called OnCreate. This method initiates the app and loads the layout page.

There are a variety of devices powered by Android, and not all of them provide the same features and capabilities. In order to prevent your application from being installed on devices that lack features needed by your application, it's important that you clearly define a profile for the types of devices your application supports by declaring device and software requirements in your manifest file.

Summary

In this chapter regarding IBM Worklight application environments, we have covered all the necessary development and deployment setups for an Android environment. Furthermore, the structure of the Android environment with all the resources has been covered in this chapter. After reading this chapter, you will be confident enough to handle the Android mobile environment and will be able to generate native mobile apps.

In the next chapter, we will look at some data handling using adapters that will be utilized for data manipulation and mapping to your application.

5
Adding an Adapter

In the previous chapter, we discussed IBM Worklight's client-side tools and their capabilities. We also discussed the range of components required to build a mobile application interface and managed to run them on real devices. In this chapter, we'll examine the Worklight's server-side **adapter** component in detail to understand how the adapters are utilized to build a connection between mobile applications and the company's backend business service for data manipulation and handling. The main purpose and reason of this chapter is to introduce you to the mechanism of data communication and handling throughout the mobile application in a heightened manner.

IBM Worklight Adapter concept

IBM Worklight Server provides us with the adapter as a way to communicate with the organization's business processes. A developer can manage to create a request to web services, REST services, and databases in a very structured way to compound information from various sources where the developer can perform necessary server-side logic on this response data to mobile devices.

Worklight Adapter works as an interpreter between mobile applications and backend enterprise systems with a flexible authentication facility to open a secure bridge between them. Moreover, adapter is developed in JavaScript and XSL, where the developer needs to write powerful server-side JavaScript code to integrate it with backend applications, and use XSL to transform hierarchical response data to JSON.

An IBM Worklight Adapter contains server-side code in its developer-defined procedures to retrieve data from the remote database and enterprise application services. Worklight Adapters are deployed on the IBM Worklight Server and can be accessed by IBM Worklight apps via a simple invocation API. Please refer to the following diagram to understand the concept of adapter calling activities in the IBM Worklight platform:

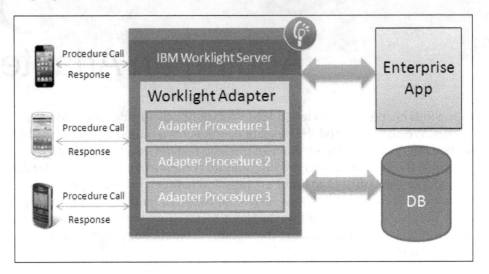

The diagram also shows a high-level view of the communication components in the Worklight platform; every adapter has the same steps for all the components:

- The mobile client creates a request to the adapter, which runs in Worklight Server

- The adapter sends this web request to destination sources such as web services and databases

- The services return the response to the adapter in an XML/JSON format

- Finally, the adapter returns the response to the mobile client in the JSON/ XML format

Exploring adapter files

A developer can use JavaScript, XML, and XSL to develop IBM Worklight Adapter, and each adapter must have following elements to run on Worklight Server:

- **The XML file**: This describes the connectivity for the backend system, to which the adapter connects and lists the procedure that is exposed by it to other adapters and applications.

- **The JavaScript file**: This contains the implementation of the procedure declared in the XML file.

- **The XSL file**: This contains zero or more XSL files, each containing a transformation from the raw XML data retrieved by the adapter. This is returned to JSON through adapter procedures.

The XML file has a main root element, `<adapter>`, and other subelements, such as `<connectivity>` and `<procedure>`, which must be declared to configure adapter in Worklight application. To get more detail on each element, please use the following IBM information center's URL:

```
http://pic.dhe.ibm.com/infocenter/wrklight/v5r0m5/index.
jsp?topic=%2Fcom.ibm.worklight.help.doc%2Fdevref%2Fr_the_adapter_xml_
file.html
```

An adapter is a collection of JavaScript functions that are remotely invoked by an application. These functions include the implementation for each procedure that is defined in the adapter.

The following list defines the procedure's rules in adapter JavaScript:

- A procedure must be declared in the adapter XML file

- The adapter JavaScript file must be used to implement the procedure's logic

- The name declared in the XML file must be used for the procedure's JavaScript function

Types of adapters

IBM Worklight provides three types of adapters to help the Worklight developer choose an appropriate adapter that depends on the developer's need and make his/her life easier with an XML configuration that has simple elements, as discussed earlier:

- HTTP adapters
- SQL adapters
- Cast Iron adapters

JavaScript is used to write the adapter code and it runs on a server on IBM Worklight's mobile application platform. IBM Worklight uses the Rhino JavaScript engine internally to run the JavaScript source code. Besides, a JMS adapter has been introduced in newer versions, which is used for messaging services and response handling.

HTTP adapters

IBM Worklight's HTTP adapter provides access to HTTP- and HTTPS-based enterprise services and is used to invoke RESTful services and SOAP-based services using the GET, POST, PUT, and DELETE methods into the request. For the response, data can be received in the XML, JSON, and HTML formats, with the content type defined in the request.

To cover the HTTP adapter example, we will use a real-time scenario by utilizing a Flickr feed RESTful service and loading data from the live server. Later on, we will manipulate this response data to utilize and create a sample demo app for Flickr in `http://www.flickr.com/services/feeds/`.

To create a HTTP adapter in the Worklight project, please perform the following steps:

1. Create a Worklight Project and name it `FlickrDemo`.

2. In the next screen, define the app name `FlickrApp`.

   We already covered the steps for this project's creation in *Chapter 3, Creating a Basic Worklight Application*, in case you have trouble creating the Worklight Project.

3. In the **Project Explorer**, right-click on the `adapter` folder and navigate to **New | Worklight Adapter**, as shown in the following screenshot:

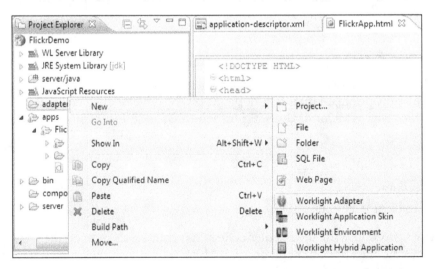

4. Select **Project name** as **FlickrDemo** from the combo, **Adapter type** as **HTTP Adapter**, and finally, enter **Adapter name** as shown in following screenshot:

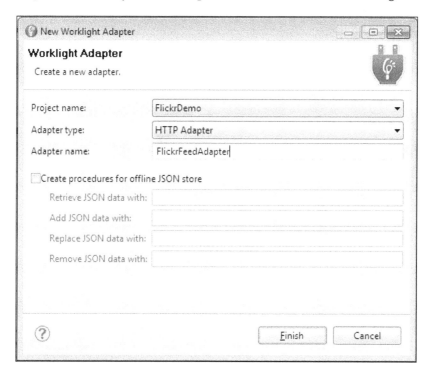

5. After clicking on **Finish**, this will generate a subfolder — the `adapter` folder. This `adapter` folder will come up with three important autogenerated files that include XML, JavaScript, and XSL, with default input text for these files. They will have the same name that we gave to the main adapter file.

6. Now we need to create a procedure declaration and configure this adapter to load the Flickr feed. Open the XML file and locate the `<connectivity>` element that holds three important elements — protocol, domain, and port. As we follow the Flickr feed's domain, we need to replace the domain value with `api.flickr.com`, where port and protocol remain same. The following code listing exposes the `<connectivity>` tag with these elements:

```
<connectivity>
<connectionPolicy xsi:type="http:HTTPConnectionPolicyType">
    <protocol>http</protocol>
    <domain>api.flickr.com</domain>
    <port>80</port>
</connectionPolicy>
<loadConstraints maxConcurrentConnectionsPerNode="2"/>
</connectivity>
```

7. Another way to configure adapter is to use **Adapter Editor.** By double-clicking on the `adapter.xml` file, the following editor will open in the IDE where you can write the adapter description as well:

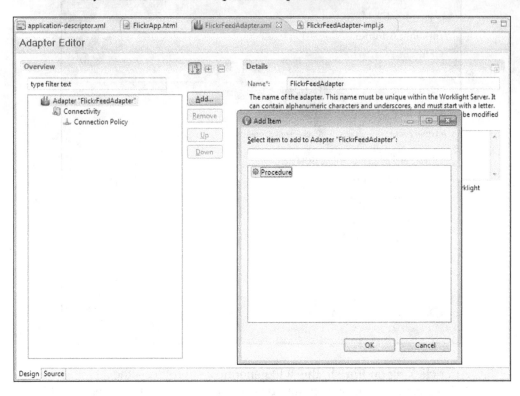

8. If you follow the wizard that was used to create the adapter, you will see two default procedures/functions with these names: `getStories` and `getStoriesFiltered`. These have already been defined in the recently developed adapter. We recommend you to remove both the procedures and add the new adapter procedure's name by using the **Add** button after selecting the adapter's root element in the left window. When you click on the **Add** button, it will open a pop-up window and select the **Procedure** item in order to add it into the adapter. The following screenshot shows you how you can add a procedure by defining a name, display, and description. You can choose any adapter name, or you can use `getFlickrFeed` to define your procedure's name.

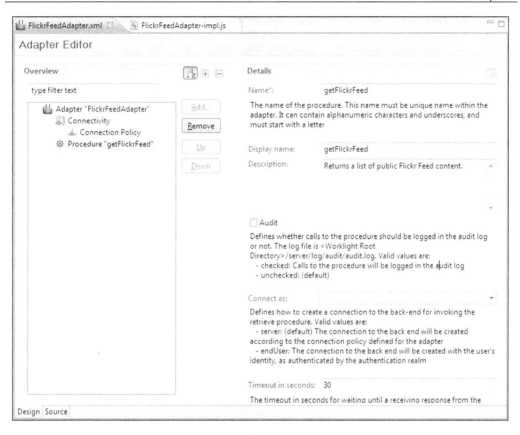

9. Once the procedure is added into the `FlickrFeedAdapter.xml` file, we are done with the declaration part. Now you must write this adapter's behavior in the JavaScript file. Open the `.js` file in the same generated `adapter` folder, remove all existing content from it, and define the function with the same procedure name that we used for the procedure. Use the following code listing and paste it into the `FlickrFeedAdapter-impl.js` file, which will later be used for the Flickr feed's request:

```
function getFlickrFeed() {
  var flickrFeedUrl =
    "/services/feeds/photos_public.gne?id=
    47906772@N05&lang=en-us&format=json";
  var input = {
    method : 'get',
    returnedContentType : 'plain',
    path : flickrFeedUrl,
  };
  var response = WL.Server.invokeHttp(input);
```

```
    var responseText = response.text;
    varres = responseText.replace("jsonFlickrFeed(", "");
    res = res.substring(0, (res.length - 1));
    res = JSON.parse(res);
    returnres;
}
```

In the preceding code listing, `var filckrFeedUrl` holds the URL to call the Flickr feed from the live site and bind it with the domain that we defined in the `FlickrFeedAdapter.xml` file. The complete URL look like this:

`http://api.flickr.com/services/feeds/photos_public.gne?id=47906772@N05&lang=en-us&format=json`

Please use following link to understand the feed's URL with all the parameter definitions in detail:

`http://www.flickr.com/services/feeds/docs/photos_public/`

The `WL.Server.invokeHttp(input)` function provided in Worklight Server API is responsible for the request/response in calling services. Now that we have done our first procedure declaration and definition, it's time to test and verify the adapter's result.

Before moving on to test the adapter's result, we need to deploy our adapter to the Worklight Sever. To do that, we also need to build our adapter to make sure that the error-free code will deploy itself into Worklight Server. In order to do that, Worklight Studio provides the Deploy Worklight Adapter the option to complete this procedure with a single click. Right-click on the `FlickrFeedAdapter` folder under the `adapter` folder and navigate to **Run As | Deploy Worklight Adapter**, as shown in the following screenshot:

Validate		
Run As	▸	1 Deploy Worklight Adapter
Debug As	▸	2 Invoke Worklight Back-end Service
Profile As	▸	3 Invoke Worklight Procedure

This will deploy the adapter on Worklight Server or check the console window for the deployment status in the Worklight Console section. Now our adapter is ready to invoke. Right-click on the `FlickrFeedAdapter` folder and navigate to **Run As | Invoke Worklight Procedure**. Clicking on it will open the pop-up **Edit Configuration and Launch** window and to invoke this, you have to select **Project name**, **Adapter name**, **Procedure name**, and **Parameters** and then click on the **Run** button.

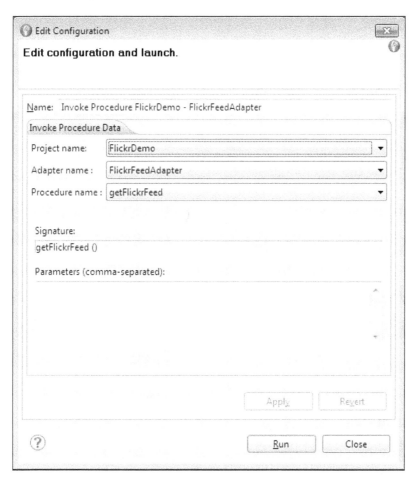

After clicking on the **Run** button, the **Invoke Procedure Result** explorer window will open in the IDE to display the results. If all the steps have been followed correctly so far, then the response that the JSON data fetched from Flickr will be displayed in the explorer window, as shown in the following screenshot:

```
Invoke Procedure Result

Invocation Result of procedure: 'getFlickrFeed' from the Worklight Server:
{
    "description": "",
    "generator": "http:\/\/www.flickr.com\/",
    "isSuccessful": true,
    "items": [
        {
            "author": "nobody@flickr.com (Adeel Ansari)",
            "author_id": "47906772@N05",
            "date_taken": "2013-07-05T20:50:44-08:00",
            "description": " <p><a href=\"http:\/\/www.flickr.com\/people\/47906772@N05\/\">Adeel
Ansari<\/a> posted a photo:<\/p> <p><a href=\"http:\/\/www.flickr.com\/photos\/47906772@N05\/9996981645\/
\" title=\"P1040773\"><img src=\"http:\/\/farm8.staticflickr.com\/7317\/9996981645_610aaa7004_m.jpg\"
width=\"240\" height=\"135\" alt=\"P1040773\" \/><\/a><\/p> ",
            "link": "http:\/\/www.flickr.com\/photos\/47906772@N05\/9996981645\/",
            "media": {
                "m": "http:\/\/farm8.staticflickr.com\/7317\/9996981645_610aaa7004_m.jpg"
            },
            "published": "2013-09-29T11:16:58Z",
            "tags": "macro",
            "title": "P1040773"
```

If you have followed the steps correctly, you will have an output that is similar to the preceding screenshot, which shows successful results from the Flickr feeds with your own created adapter.

SQL adapters

IBM Worklight SQL adapter is designed to interact with any SQL data source and is used to execute plain parameterized SQL queries and stored procedures to retrieve and update data in the databases. Currently, Worklight SQL adapter supports the following databases:

- MySQL
- Oracle 11g
- DB2

The JDBC connector driver for a specific database type can be downloaded from the MySQL, DB2, and Oracle websites. The developer will have to add a specific driver jar into the `server` | `lib` folder under Worklight project directory structure to make it available to the app.

To get a clearer idea about the SQL adapter, we will include an exercise for you to authenticate a user by matching the user credentials from the database. Through this exercise, you will learn two basic things that include database connection and performing a SQL using the SQL adapter. Creating a SQL adapter's steps is very much similar to an HTTP adapter.

Before diving into the creation of a SQL adapter, we would like you to have an in-depth understanding of the SQL adapter, regarding its files and configuration elements. A SQL adapter mainly has two important files—one is the `.xml` file that is used to configure the data source and declare the procedures, and another is the JavaScript for the definition of the declared procedures. The `.xml` file has the `<connectionPolicy>` element under `<connectivity>`, which is used to configure the connection type for an adapter. For a SQL adapter, a mandatory attribute `xsi:type` must be set to a `sql:SQLConnectionPolicy` value.

The `<connnectionPolicy>` element provides you with two choices to connect with the database. One is the `<datasourceDefinition>` subelement that is used to define the data source and the other is the `<dataSourceJNDIName>` subelement that is used for the JNDI Name of the data source provided by the application server.

To use the `<dataSourceDefinition>` subelement, the following elements must be defined:

* `driverClass`: This is used to load the driver class; for example, `com.mysql.jdbc.Drive`.
* `url`: This is used to specify the data source such as `"jdbc.mysql://localhost:3306/dbName`.
* `user`: This is used to specify the username that is used to access the database.
* `password`: This is used to specify the database's user password.

The following code listing shows us the structure of the preceding elements with their configuration:

```
<connectivity>
<connectionPolicyxsi:type="sql:SQLConnectionPolicy">
<dataSourceDefinition>
  <driverClass>com.mysql.jdbc.Driver</driverClass>
  <url>jdbc:mysql://localhost:3306/dbName</url>
  <user>myPassword</user>
<password>myPassword</password>
  </dataSourceDefinition>
</connectionPolicy>
<loadConstraints maxConcurrentConnectionsPerNode="5"/>
</connectivity>
```

Declaring the procedure in a SQL adapter is same as an HTTP adapter, where a `.js` file is used to define the SQL statement that executes under a procedure/function. To create a SQL statement, Worklight Server API has a `WL.Server.createSQLStatement` method and to invoke this SQL statement, the same Server API has the `WL.Server.invokeSQLStatement` function.

Later in this chapter, we will discuss both the functions in detail and implement the creation of the SQL adapter's steps.

We will assume that you already have a database setup in your machine and to use Worklight SQL adapter, we need to have a schema ready to test and run it. The following code is a SQL script for the database and table that we have used in our example:

```
CREATE SCHEMA `FlickrDemo`;

CREATE TABLE `FlickrDemo`. `Authentication` (
  `username` VARCHAR (50) NOT NULL,
  `password` VARCHAR (50) NOT NULL ,
`first_name` VARCHAR (45) NULL,
  `last_name` VARCHAR (45) NULL,
  UNIQUE INDEX `username_UNIQUE` (`username` ASC));
```

For the table data, use the following queries to prepare the record for the table that will be created:

```
INSERT INTO `FlickrDemo`. `authentication` (`username`,
  `password`,`first_name`,`last_name`)VALUES('talhaH',
  '123456','Talha', 'Haroon' );

INSERT INTO `FlickrDemo`. `authentication` (`username`,`password`,
  `first_name`,`last_name`)VALUES  ('saifo', '123456',
  'Muhammad', 'Saifuddin');
```

Let's use the following steps to create a SQL adapter:

1. In **Project Explorer**, right-click on the adapter folder, navigate to **New | Worklight Adapter**, and use following screenshot to fill up the values for each required field:

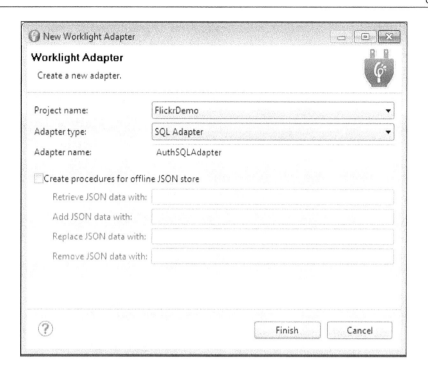

2. Use **Adapter type SQL Adapter** and define **Adapter name**, and click on the **Finish** button. This will generate AuthSQLAdapter under the adapter folder with two files—one is .xml and other is a .js file.

3. Now open the .xml file; you'll find that the default code is written for you to configure the database source and procedure definition; we will follow the same code with slight changes. You can use the following code to make changes if you follow the same values into the new generated adapter .xml file:

```
<connectivity>
<connectionPolicyxsi:type="sql:SQLConnectionPolicy">
<dataSourceDefinition>
   <driverClass>com.mysql.jdbc.Driver</driverClass>
   <url>jdbc:mysql://localhost:3306/flickrDemo</url>
   <user>root</user>
<password>root</password>
   </dataSourceDefinition>
</connectionPolicy>
<loadConstraints maxConcurrentConnectionsPerNode="5"/>
</connectivity>
```

4. Defining the procedure in `adapter.xml` is the same as the procedure in an HTTP adapter. As we use this database connection to authenticate the user, we declare the procedure with the `authenticateUser` name, as shown in the following code:

```
<procedure name="authenticateUser"/>
```

5. Now, open the `adapter.js` file to define the function with the same name that we used to declare in the `adapter.xml` file to implement the procedure logic. Don't forget the rules that we have mentioned earlier to define a procedure in the adapter JavaScript file. You can copy the following code and paste it the `adapter.js` file to follow up this example:

```
var procedure1Statement = WL.Server.createSQLStatement
  ("select * from authentication where username =?
  AND password =?");

Function authenticateUser(username, password) {
  return WL.Server.invokeSQLStatement ({
    preparedStatement : procedure1Statement,
    Parameters: [username, password]
  });
}
```

As shown in the preceding code, `WL.Server.createSQLStatmenet` is used to create the SQL query; in this query, we will authenticate the user by matching the username and password. A SQL statement's object must always be defined outside the function. The second most important function used in the `authnticateUser` function is `WL.Server.invokeSQLStatement`. This is used to invoke SQL statement/queries and returns the result to the application or procedure caller.

6. It's time to test what we have done so far before we deploy the adapter on the server. In order to do this, we can use the same adapter deployment and invoke the steps that we used in the HTTP adapter. When the **Invoke Adapter** option is selected, the pop-up window will appear as shown in the following screenshot:

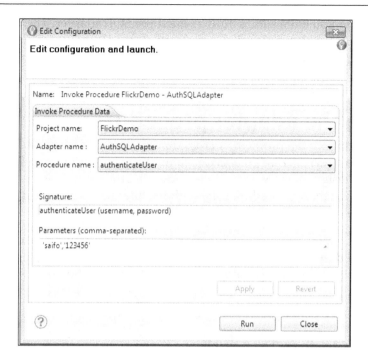

7. I hope that you're already familiar with the screen of the procedure's call and selection at this stage. As this makes sense to you, we will also provide a parameter as our procedure accepts two arguments to invoke this procedure. So move on and click on **Run**; this will open the **Invoke Procedure Result** explorer window in the IDE with the result as shown in the following screenshot:

```
AuthSQLAdapter.xml    AuthSQLAdapter-impl.js    Invoke Procedure Result

Invocation Result of procedure: 'authenticateUser' from the Worklight Server:
{
    "isSuccessful": true,
    "resultSet": [
        {
            "first_name": "Muhammad",
            "last_name": "Saifuddin",
            "password": "123456",
            "username": "saifo"
        }
    ]
}
```

Congratulations! You have successfully created the SQL adapter. The result is retrieved as a JSON object where it is a property named `isSuccessful`, as shown in the preceding screenshot, pointing out that the invocation was successful and `resultSet` is an array of returned database records.

Invoking the adapter procedure

In general, we do face the problem of cross domain/origin security issues when making a call to a server from JavaScript. Here, IBM Worklight's application architecture is designed in a way to avoid these constraints so that the developer can easily manage these procedure calls with the adapters that are deployed on IBM Worklight Server.

The `WL.Client.invokeProcedure` function invokes the adapter's procedure that has been exposed by an IBM Worklight Client API. This function accepts two parameters, the first one is mandatory and second one is optional, as shown in the following code:

```
WL.Client.invokeProcedure(invocationData, options)
```

The parameter's details are listed as follows:

- `invocationData`: This contains three configuration parameters—the adapter name, procedure name, and parameters to be passed as JSON objects.

- `options`: This is an optional parameter that is passed as a standard option object and defines different properties, which are listed as follows:

  - `timeout`: This accepts an integer number of milliseconds, which will be used to wait for the server's response before it fails with a request timeout.

  - `onSuccess`: This is a success handler used for a callback function to receive the data in a standard response object. The `isSuccessful` attribute of the `invocationResult` property is true.

  - `onFailure`: This is a failure handler used for a callback function to receive a standard response object with technical failure. This resulted in the same `invocationResult` property, with the `isSuccessful` attribute set to true.

The `InvocationData` parameter syntax must be the same as the following JSON block:

```
var invocationData = {
  adapter : 'AdapterOne', // adapter name
  procedure : 'procedureOne', // procedure name
  parameters : [] // parameters if any
};
```

To invoke a procedure from the client application, the `WL.Client.invokeProcedure` function is used to hit the request, which takes the `invocationData` and both success and failure callback methods. The syntax that is used to call the adapter procedure using the `invokeProcedure` method will be like the following code:

```
WL.Client.invokeProcedure(invocationData, {
  onSuccess: handleSuccess,
  onFailure: handleFailure,
});

function handleSuccess(result){
  WL.Logger.debug(JSON.stringify(result));
}

function handleFailure(result){
  WL.Logger.debug(JSON.stringify(result));
}
```

When the adapter's procedure is invoked by the `invocationResult` property that is included in the response, which is received on both success and failure handler functions. Furthermore, this invocationResult property has one more attribute defined with the name `isSuccesful`, which represents the Boolean data type. This isSuccessful attribute contains the true value when the procedure invocation is successful or is false when the procedure invocation fails.

Calling Java code using an adapter

Worklight Adapter is a server-side entity and the adapter is implemented in JavaScript, where the developer is limited to performing complex functions such as data encryption, accessing and maintaining disturbed directory information such as the **Lightweight Directory Access Protocol (LDAP)**, custom or utility API's such as iText to generate a PDF document, and so on. As most of the available utility libraries are commonly written in Java and PHP languages, JavaScript is not enough to handle these kind of features. To overcome this issue, IBM Worklight provides us with a way to write Java code within the application and calls it from the adapter using the JavaScript code.

To write the Java code, Worklight provides us with the `java` folder within the `server` directory. Moreover, IBM Worklight Studio automatically builds the Java files and deploys them to the IBM Worklight Server.

Note that the developer will have to declare the package to add a Java class into the project, and the package name must start with `com`, `org`, or `net` to be defined under the Worklight project.

To demonstrate this concept, we will create a Java class and define a method that accepts a string and converts it into a hashcode using MD5 algorithm. Using the adapter function, we will this hits java method, which returns the hashcode of the given input.

1. In the first step, we need to create the `java` class in the `server/java` folder under the Worklight Project, as shown in the following screenshot.

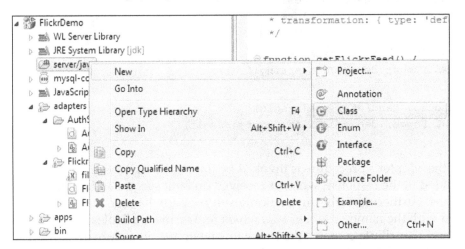

2. Selecting **Class** from menu will open the class' definition window. Please note a few things in the following screenshot—you must define any **Package** name that starts with `com`, `net`, or `org` and declare the class name with any name you like, or you can use the same values that we used in the following screenshot:

3. When you click on **Finish**, the blank class is created in the `server/java` folder. Open this file and paste the following code snippet into it:

```
package com.demo.util;

import java.security.MessageDigest;
import java.security.NoSuchAlgorithmException;

public class DemoUtil {

  public String convertHash (String password) {
    StringBuffer sb = null;
  try {
    MessageDigest md = MessageDigest.getInstance("MD5");
    md.update(password.getBytes());
```

```
        byte byteData[] = md.digest();
        sb = new StringBuffer();
        for (int i = 0; i < byteData.length; i++) {
            sb.append(Integer.toString((byteData[i] & 0xff)
                + 0x100, 16).substring(1));
        }
    } catch (NoSuchAlgorithmException e) {
        e.printStackTrace();
    }
    return sb.toString();
    }
}
```

This DemoUtil class has only one method name, convertHash, which is used to accept the string type's value and convert this hashcode using the MD5 algorithm and finally return the converted string to the caller.

Invoking Java code from the adapter

To invoke this Java code, we add the procedure into the same HTTP adapter with the testJavaCode name in the adapter.xml file, as shown in the following code:

```
<procedure name="testJavaCode"></procedure>
```

Now, add the function in the same adapter.js file and if you're following the same example, you can paste the following code into your adapter.js file:

```
function testJavaCode() {
    var obj = new com.demo.util.DemoUtil();
    return { result : obj.convertHash("123456"),}
}
```

First, we create the object of our class with a fully qualified name using a package and then we call the class method covertHash using the same object, passing a string value. Finally, we return the JSON format result.

Now, follow the same steps to deploy and invoke the adapter's procedure using the IDE option, select the testJavaCode procedure in the procedure combo in the **Edit Configuration and Launch** window, and click on **Run**. This will print a result that will be similar to the following listing in the **Invoke Procedure Result** explorer window:

```
{
    "isSuccessful": true,
    "result": "e10adc3949ba59abbe56e057f20f883e"
}
```

Summary

So far, we have covered and understood the power of adapters in Worklight with its different types provided by the IBM Worklight bundle and figured out how each adapter's type can be utilized between mobile and enterprise applications to deliver data between them. We also saw how IBM Worklight proves itself to be the best and easiest way to interact with backend services and databases using an adapter with an efficient client code in JavaScript. In the next chapter, we will cover another core topic of how to apply security while transmitting data between the enterprise and mobile application for the authorized user.

6
Authentication and Security

So far, we have covered data handling using multiple features and techniques of mobile and enterprise data applications by using SQL and HTTP adapters. In this chapter, we will explore the security capabilities of IBM Worklight.

We can protect our applications and adapter procedures against unauthorized access request and transfer secure data between mobile and enterprise applications. We will also learn about the general security principles, concepts, and terminologies.

Worklight has a built-in authentication framework that allows the developer to configure and use it with very little effort. The Worklight project has an authentication configuration file, which is used to declare and force security on mobile applications, adapters, data, and web resources, which consist of the following security entities.

We will talk about the various predefined authentication realms and security tests that are provided in Worklight out of the box.

To identify the importance of mobile security, you can see that in today's life, we keep our personal and business data on mobile devices. The data and applications are both important to us. Both the data and applications should be protected against unauthorized access, particularly if they contain sensitive information, which is transmitted over the network. There are number of ways via which a device can be compromised, and it can leak data to malicious users.

Worklight security principles, concepts, and terminologies

IBM Worklight provides various security roles to protect applications, adapter procedures, and static resources from an unauthorized access.

Each role can be defined by a **security test** that comprises one or more authentication realms. The authentication realm defines a process that will be used to authenticate the users.

The authentication realm has the following parts:

- **Challenge handler**: This is a component on the device side

- **Authenticator and login module**: This is a component on the server

  One authentication realm can be used to protect multiple resources. We will look into each component in detail.

- **Device Request Flow**: The following screenshot shows a device that makes a request to access a protected resource, for example, an adapter function, on the server. In response to the request, the server sends back an authentication challenge to the device to submit its authenticity:

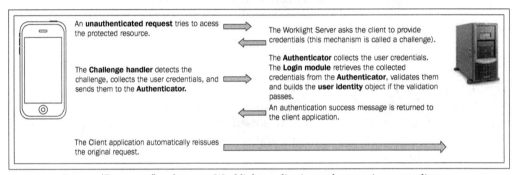

Request/Response flow between Worklight application and enterprise server diagram

Challenge handler

The challenge handler component is written in JavaScript, and it is used to control the authentication process. Whenever WL Server sends a response, challenge handler is responsible to detect any possible authentication challenge that the server has sent over to it. Once a challenge handler has detected an authentication challenge that has come from the server, it will collect the required credentials on the device and will send them back to the server for further processing.

For example, a user is trying to access a protected adapter function, let's say a database record. WL Server will automatically detect this action and return a challenge to the device to prove its authenticity. Now, when the response comes back to the device, a challenge handler will further process it by collecting credentials and sending them back to the WL Server.

There can be multiple challenge handler instances for each realm application that needs to be authenticated. When an authentication flow is completed, the challenge handler sends a notification back to the Worklight framework indicating whether the authentication was a success or a failure.

There are some predefined methods that you will use to create a challenge handler and submit credentials back to the WL Server. We will learn about them later.

Authenticator

The authenticator component is written in the Java language and exists on the server side. It is used to collect the credentials sent by a client application. The credentials are passed on to a login module for validation. It can be used to collect any type of information accessible from an HTTP request object — cookies, headers, body, or any other properties. One authenticator type can be used by multiple authentication realms.

The following diagram shows how the same authenticator type can be used for several realms.

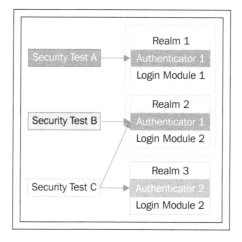

These are the three predefined authenticators present in Worklight Server:

- **Adapter-based authenticator**: This authenticator is implemented via adapter procedures to collect and validate credentials from the client application.

- **Form-based authenticator**: This authenticator sends a challenge in the form of an HTML login form to clients. It is useful for both web environments as well as mobile applications.

- **Header-based authenticator**: This authenticator does not check for interactive credentials' collection but is used to check for specific HTTP headers.

In addition to a predefined authenticator, a user can create his or her own authenticator components in Java.

The login module

A login module exists on the WL Server, and it is used to verify the user credentials and then create a user identity object, which contains the user properties throughout the life of the session.

Validation of credentials can be done in various ways, for example:

- Through a web service
- By looking up the user in a user's table in a database
- By using the WebSphere® LTPA token

It is possible to add custom properties in the user identity object according to your specific needs. The login module is also responsible to destroy the user identity object once the session has been terminated. It can be configured to automatically record login attempts for audit purposes. A login module can be used by multiple authentication realms.

Similar to the custom authenticator, it is also possible to create your own custom login module in Java.

Authentication realms

An authentication realm comprises a challenge handler, authenticator, login module, and a definition of the authentication process. One authentication realm can be used by more than one security test. Each authentication realm defines its flow as shown in the following diagram:

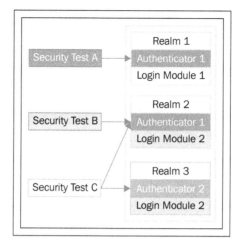

Each authentication realm has one authenticator and one login module only.

The following are some questions of the flow:

- Once the authentication process has been triggered, what should happen next?
- What type of challenge should it send back to the client application?
- If a request arrives from a device, what credentials should it collect from it?
- How and when should the credentials be collected?
- How should the credentials be validated and sent to the server?
- What will be the result of the credentials' validation?
- What will be the properties of the user identity object?

There are several predefined authentication realms available in Worklight, for instance, remote application disable or an application authenticity.

Security test

A security test is created with an ordered set of authentication realms that are used to protect a resource such as an adapter procedure, an application, or a static URL. Security test defines one or more realms against which users must have to authenticate in order to access backed adapter function or resource. If multiple realms have been used, then the developer has to define the order in which the authentication should be performed.

You can create custom security tests along with default security tests that you can use for mobile and web environments' protection. The following diagram shows multiple security tests:

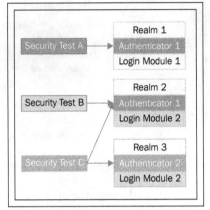

A security test can use more than one realm, and one realm can be used for multiple security tests.

Examining generated realms, security test, and login modules

Realms, security tests, and login modules are defined in the `authenticationConfig.xml` file located at the `server/conf` folder of a Worklight project.

Open your Worklight project and locate the `authenticationConfig.xml` file and check for the following entries that are present by default to help you quick start with it:

Worklight application's authenticationConfig.xml file's location

Let's create a new Worklight project and examine what realms, security tests, and login modules are generated for us by default.

Generating realms

We can see that the following realms have been generated by default, which we can use or customize further:

```
<realms>
  <realm name="SampleAppRealm" loginModule="StrongDummy">
  <className>com.worklight.core.auth.ext.FormBasedAuthenticator
    </className>
  </realm>
  <realm name="WorklightConsole" loginModule="requireLogin">
  <className>com.worklight.core.auth.ext.FormBasedAuthenticator
    </className>
   <onLoginUrl>/console</onLoginUrl>
  </realm>
</realms>
```

Generating login modules

We can see that the following login modules have been generated by default, which we can use or customize further:

```
<loginModules>
 <loginModule name="StrongDummy">
  <className>com.worklight.core.auth.ext.NonValidatingLoginModule
    </className>
 </loginModule>
 <loginModule name="requireLogin">
  <className>com.worklight.core.auth.ext.SingleIdentityLoginModule
    </className>
 </loginModule>
</loginModules>
```

Generating security tests

We can see that the following security tests have been generated by default, which we can use or customize further:

```
<securityTests>
    <customSecurityTest name="WorklightConsole">
      <test realm="WorklightConsole" isInternalUserID="true"/>
    </customSecurityTest>
```

```
                <mobileSecurityTest name="mobileTests">
                  <testAppAuthenticity/>
                  <testDeviceId provisioningType="none" />
                  <testUser realm="myMobileLoginForm" />
                </mobileSecurityTest>
           <webSecurityTest name="webTests">
                  <testUser realm="myWebLoginForm"/>
                </webSecurityTest>
           <customSecurityTest name="customTests">
                      <test realm="wl_antiXSRFRealm" step="1"/>
                      <test realm="wl_authenticityRealm" step="1"/>
                      <test realm="wl_remoteDisableRealm" step="1"/>
                  <test realm="wl_anonymousUserRealm" isInternalUserID="true"
           step="1"/>
                      <test realm="wl_deviceNoProvisioningRealm"
           isInternalDeviceID="true" step="2"/>
           </customSecurityTest>
           </securityTests>
```

Creating adapter-based authentication

Adapter-based authentication is the simplest form of authentication provided in Worklight. It uses the `adapter` procedure/function to validate and authenticate the users and create their sessions. Plus, it provides all the features of the Worklight authentication framework.

Please use the following simple steps to implement adapter-based authentication:

1. Create a new Worklight project with the name `ABADemo`; for the application, use the name `myAdapterBasedAuthentication`.

2. Add an adapter and give it a name: `myAuthAdapter`. Paste the following sample function code into the `adapter.js` file:

```
function onAuthRequired(headers, errorMessage){
  errorMessage = errorMessage ? errorMessage : null;
  return {
    authRequired: true,
    errorMessage: errorMessage
  };
}

function submitUserAuthentication(username, password){
  if (username==="adapter" && password === "adapter"){
    var userIdentity = {
```

```
          userId: username,
          displayName: username,
          attributes: {
            foo: "abc"
          }
        };
        WL.Server.setActiveUser("myAuthRealm", userIdentity);
        return {
          authRequired: false
        };
    }
    return onAuthRequired(null, "Invalid login credentials,
      please try again");
}

function getSomeData(){
    return {
      secretData: "This is sample data retruned after user
        session creation"
    };
}

function onLogout(){
    WL.Server.setActiveUser("myAuthRealm", null);
    WL.Logger.debug("Logged out");
}
```

I hope that the preceding code with so many function names make sense to you. If it doesn't, lets go through each function in detail:

- ○ submitUserAuthentication: This function is used to authenticate the users and create sessions (user identity objects). The username and password are received from the application as parameters. If a validation is successfully passed, a WL.Server.setActiveUser API is called to create an authenticated session for myAuthRealm with a user data stored in the userIdentity object. Note, you can add your own custom properties to user identity attributes.

- ○ onAuthRequired: This function is used to return a success or failure response back to the client. Note the authRequired: true property. You need this property in the challenge handler to detect that either the server is requesting authentication or not.

- getSomeData: This is a function that is protected with a security test and only authenticated users can access it. So, in this case, once the user has successfully passed the authentication defined in the preceding function, then this function will be called.

- onLogout: This function will be called when the session times out, either explicitly by the user or once the session timeout duration has finished.

3. Locate the authenticationconfig.xml file and add the following entries into it.

- Add a new realm and login module as follows:

```xml
<realms>
  <realm loginModule="myAuthLoginModule"
name="myAdapterAuthRealm">
    <className>com.worklight.integration.auth.
AdapterAuthenticator</className>
    <parameter name="login-function" value="myAuthAdapter.
onAuthRequired"/>
    <parameter name="logout-function" value="myAuthAdapter.
onLogout"/>
  </realm>
</realms>
<loginModules>
  <loginModule name="myAuthLoginModule">
    <className>com.worklight.core.auth.ext.
NonValidatingLoginModule</className>
  </loginModule>
</loginModules>
```

- myAdapterAuthRealm: This is the realm that we have created. The class type of this realm is AdapterAuthentication. There are two parameters defined, one is login-function that is called at the time of user login (authentication step) and the second function, logout-function is called when session is going to expire.

- myAuthLoginModule: This is the login module that we will use. The type of module is NonValidatingLoginModule, and it means it will not further validates user's credentials and the developer will take the whole responsibility of validating credentials inside the adapter.

4. Add the security test as follows:

- Add the following security test to the authenticationconfig.xml file. You must use this security test to protect the adapter procedure, so convert it into <customSecurityTest>:

```
<securityTests>
    <customSecurityTest name="myAuthAdapter-securityTest">
        <test isInternalUserID="true" realm="myAuthRealm"/>
    </customSecurityTest>
</securityTests>
```

5. Now open the adapter XML file `myAuthAdapter.xml` and add the security test as follows:

```
<procedure name="submitUserAuthentication"/>
<procedure name="getSomeData" securityTest=
  "myAuthAdapter-securityTest"/>
```

°   The `submitUserAuthentication` procedure is used to trigger the authentication process, and authentication is not required in order to invoke it.

°   The second procedure is accessible to authenticated users only because we have protected it with a security test.

The following diagram shows the adapter-based authentication process:

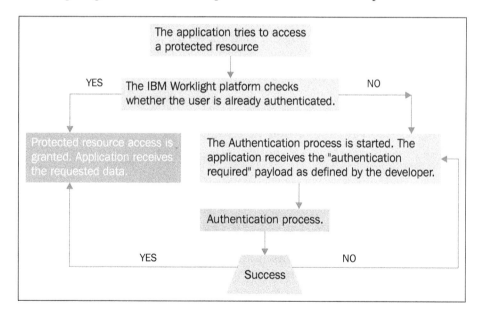

Client side – adapter authentication components

In this section, we are going to create a client-side interface to manipulate this authentication concept:

1. Create an app, give it the name `myAdapterBasedAuthentication`, and paste the following code in the HTML file in the `common` folder under the `body` tag:

```
<div id="MainAppDiv">
<div class="header">
    <h1>my Adapter Based Authentication App</h1>
  </div>
</div>
<div id="AuthDiv" style="display:none">
</div>
```

The page contains two div elements: the `MainAppDiv` is used to display the application content, and the `AuthDiv` is used for the authentication form purposes.

When the app starts, it will hide `MainAppDiv` and will only show `AuthDiv` because the user has not logged in to access the protected data from the server. So, once the user enters the correct credentials, `AuthDiv` gets hidden and `MainAppDiv` becomes visible.

2. Let's create two buttons. One button will access the protected adapter function to get protected data and the second button will log out the user. Add the following lines inside the `MainAppDiv`:

```
<input type="button" value="Get personal details"
  onclick="getSomeData()" />
<input type="button" value="Logout"
  onclick="WL.Client.logout('myAuthRealm', {onSuccess:WL.Client.
reloadApp})" />
          <div id="ResponseDiv"></div>
```

3. The div with the ID `ResponseDiv` is used to display the `getSomeData` response. Add the following lines to `AuthDiv`:

```
<p id="AuthInfo"></p>
<hr />
<input type="text" placeholder="Enter username"
  id="AuthUsername"/><br />
<input type="password" placeholder="Enter password"
  id="AuthPassword"/><br />
```

```
<input type="button" value="Submit" id="AuthSubmitButton"
 />
<input type="button" value="Cancel" id="AuthCancelButton"
 />
```

- ° The AuthInfo tag is used to display error messages
- ° The AuthUsername and AuthPassword tags are used to input username and password respectively
- ° The AuthSubmitButton tag is used to trigger the login click event, and the AuthCancelButton tag is used to cancel the login event

In the next section, we will be creating a challenge handler component.

Challenge handler in Worklight

A challenge handler is a client-side component, located on the device. It is responsible for detecting an authentication challenge from a server, or when an authentication request from the server allows a developer to create a customized authentication process by collecting credentials and sending them back to the server as its response. Each challenge handler identifies the authentication realm to which it applies. To create a challenge handler, refer to the following section.

Create a JavaScript file that contains the following piece of code. This is the challenge handler component, and it is responsible to bring data from the server and handle the authentication challenge response whenever it arrives from the server:

```
var myAuthRealmChallengeHandler = WL.Client.createChallengeHandler("my
AuthRealm"); //line# 01

myAuthRealmChallengeHandler.isCustomResponse = function(response) { //
line# 03
  if (!response || !response.responseJSON  || response.responseText
=== null) {
    return false;
  }
  if (typeof(response.responseJSON.authRequired) !==
  'undefined'){
    return true;
  } else {
    return false;
  }
};

myAuthRealmChallengeHandler.handleChallenge = function(response){ //
line# 15
```

```
    var authRequired = response.responseJSON.authRequired;

    if (authRequired == true){ //line# 18
      $("#MainAppDiv").hide();
      $("#AuthDiv").show();
      $("#AuthPassword").empty();
      $("#AuthInfo").empty();

      if (response.responseJSON.errorMessage)
          $("#AuthInfo").html(new Date() + " :: " + response.
responseJSON.errorMessage);

    } else if (authRequired == false){
      $("#MainAppDiv").show();
      $("#AuthDiv").hide();
      myAuthRealmChallengeHandler.submitSuccess();//line# 30
    }
  };

$("#AuthSubmitButton").bind('click', function () {
  var username = $("#AuthUsername").val();
  var password = $("#AuthPassword").val();

  var invocationData = {
    adapter : "myAuthAdapter",
    procedure : "submitUserAuthentication",
    parameters : [ username, password ]
  };
  myAuthRealmChallengeHandler.submitAdapterAuthentication(invocationDa
ta, {}); //line# 42
});

$("#AuthCancelButton").bind('click', function () {
  $("#MainAppDiv").show();
  $("#AuthDiv").hide();
  myAuthRealmChallengeHandler.submitFailure();//line# 48
});
```

Now let's examine the preceding code:

- The first line # `01` is about creating a challenge handler object, and it is achieved via the `WL.Client.createChallengeHandler()` API call. A realm name must be supplied as a parameter. In our case, we have created the realm `myAuthRealm`.

- The defined `isCustomResponse` function on line # 03 of the challenge handler is called each time a response is received from the server. It is used to detect whether the response contains data that is related to this challenge handler. It returns either `true` or `false`.

- If the `isCustomResponse` function returns `true`, the framework calls the `handleChallenge()` function defined on the line # 15. This function is used to perform the required actions, such as hiding the application screen and showing the login screen. The challenge handler provides the following functionalities that you may need to use:

    ○ The `myChallengeHandler.submitAdapterAuthentication()` function coded on line # 42 is used to send the collected credentials to a specific adapter procedure. It has the same signature as the `WL.Client.invokeProcedure()` API.

    ○ The `myChallengeHandler.submitSuccess()` function call on line # 30 is used to notify the Worklight framework that the authentication has finished successfully. The Worklight framework then automatically issues the original request that triggers the authentication.

    ○ The `myChallengeHandler.submitFailure()` function call on line # 48 is used to notify the Worklight framework that the authentication has failed. The Worklight framework then disposes the original request that triggers the authentication.

- On line # 18, if `authRequires` is `true`, it shows a login screen, cleans up the password field, and shows an `errorMessage` (if present).

- If `authRequired` is `false`, it shows `MainAppDiv`, hides `AuthDiv`, and it notifies the Worklight framework that the authentication is successfully completed.

When the user clicks on the login button, it triggers the function that collects the username and the password from the HTML input fields and submits them to the adapter. Notice that we have used the `submitAdapterAuthentication` method of the challenge handler.

Form-based authentication

Form-based authentication is similar to a web application in which the users have to fill out a login form in order to access a secured or protected resource. Worklight provides a similar authentication mechanism in which the server returns the HTML of a login form whenever an application tries to access a protected resource.

The Worklight application that uses form-based authentication must use a login module to validate the received credentials.

Security realm

Declare the security realm with the name myFormBasedAppRealm as follows:

```
<realm name="myFormBasedAppRealm" loginModule="myFormBasedAppLoginMod
ule">
  <className>com.worklight.core.auth.ext.FormBasedAuthenticator</
className>
</realm>
```

The login module

Now define the login module with the name myFormBasedAppLoginModule as we used the same for the loginModule attribute value to define the realm:

```
<loginModule name="myFormBasedAppLoginModule">
  <className>com.worklight.core.auth.ext.NonValidatingLoginModule</
className>
</loginModule>
```

Security test

Declare the security test name with the name myFormBasedAppSecurityTest, and define the declared realm under the test tag:

```
<customSecurityTest name="myFormBasedAppSecurityTest">
        <test realm="myFormBasedAppRealm" isInternalUserID="true"/>
</customSecurityTest>
```

Challenge handler

Now creating a challenge handler for form-based authentication is similar to the previous example with few changes to handle the challenge for form-based authentication. Following is the code to create form-based authentication:

```
var sampleAppRealmChallengeHandler =
  WL.Client.createChallengeHandler("myFormBasedAppRealm"); //line
    # 01

sampleAppRealmChallengeHandler.isCustomResponse =
  function(response) {
    if (!response || response.responseText === null) {
```

```
          return false;
    }
    var indicatorIdx = response.responseText.search('j_security_
check');

    if (indicatorIdx >= 0){
    return true;
    }
  return false;
};


sampleAppRealmChallengeHandler.handleChallenge =
  function(response) {
  $('#MainAppBody').hide();
  $('#AuthBody').show();
  $('#passwordInputField').val('');
};


sampleAppRealmChallengeHandler.submitLoginFormCallback =
  function(response) {
    var isLoginFormResponse =
      sampleAppRealmChallengeHandler.isCustomResponse(response);
    if (isLoginFormResponse){
      sampleAppRealmChallengeHandler.handleChallenge(response);
    } else {
    $('#MainAppBody').show();
    $('#AuthBody').hide();
    sampleAppRealmChallengeHandler.submitSuccess();
    }
};


$('#loginButton').bind('click', function () {
    var reqURL = '/j_security_check';
    var options = {};
    options.parameters = {
        j_username : $('#usernameInputField').val(),
        j_password : $('#passwordInputField').val()
    };
    options.headers = {};
    sampleAppRealmChallengeHandler.submitLoginForm(reqURL,
      options,
        sampleAppRealmChallengeHandler.submitLoginFormCallback);
});


$('#cancelButton').bind('click', function () {
```

```
        sampleAppRealmChallengeHandler.submitFailure();
        $('#MainAppBody').show();
        $('#AuthBody').hide();
    });
```

If you see, we have first created an instance of a challenge handler as we did in adapter-based authentication. After that, in the `isCustomResponse` function, we search for the `j_security_check` string. If it exists, it means a login form has been sent by the server and the challenge handler will return `true`.

- The following line shows:

  ```
  var isLoginFormResponse =
    sampleAppRealmChallengeHandler.isCustomResponse(response);
  ```

- The callback function will check the response for the containing server challenge again. If the challenge is found, the `handleChallenge()` function is invoked again.

- The `handleChallenge()` function will again show a login form to the user to re-enter the correct credentials.

- Otherwise, `sampleAppRealmChallengeHandler.submitSuccess();` will be called to let the Worklight framework know that the challenge has been handled successfully, and it can proceed with the original request of the user.

If the user wants to terminate the authentication validation process and also wants to reject the original request that had triggered the authentication, he or she has to call `sampleAppRealmChallengeHandler.submitFailure();`.

Custom authentication

It is possible that these Worklight-provided authentications do not fulfill your requirements. In such scenarios, Worklight provides you with an ability to create custom realms, login modules, and security tests based on your specific needs.

In this case, you will create your custom Java class that implements the `WorkLightAuthenticator` interface in order to create an authenticator. Similar to creating a custom login module, you need to extend the `WorkLightLoginModule` interface.

The login module will create a request object that contains the user ID and password, and based on the user-specified validation, it will create a user identity object, that is, a session object.

For more information on custom authentication, please refer to IBM Worklight Info Centre (`http://pic.dhe.ibm.com/infocenter/wrklight/v5r0m6/index.jsp?topic=%2Fcom.ibm.help.doc%2Fwl_home.html`).

Summary

In this chapter, we learned about Worklight security concepts, Worklight authentication processes, and various options to protect mobile applications, adapters, and resources. We briefly talked about various authentication mechanisms such as the ones that are adapter based, form based, and custom authentications.

We learnt how to implement adapter-based authentication in a Worklight application. We worked on an example by creating adapter-based authentication and examined the steps that an authentication process goes through. Moreover, we slightly touched form-based authentication and custom authentications as well. In the next chapter, we will be coming across some of the most advanced features and extensions, including push notifications, WL APIs, Cordova plugins, and offline cache mechanism, which allows you to extend your mobile application.

7
Advanced Features of IBM Worklight

In this chapter, we will cover some advanced topics and provide you with complete knowledge of the implementation of features detailed here. If we summarize what we have covered so far, then we'd realize that we have worked on the basics of IBM Worklight. This includes components, frameworks, client- or server-side development, UI implementation, configuration, and development of IBM Worklight application and authentication concepts. Now, we will move on to some advanced development concepts using IBM Worklight Studio, which contains the WL Client API, a push notification mechanism, Cordova plugins, some UI common controls, encrypted cache, offline access, and JSONStore.

As you know, Worklight doesn't provide a proprietary development language or any model that the user has to learn specifically. It simply uses web technologies such as HTML, JavaScript, and CSS to implement IBM Worklight, a development concept of the hybrid mobile application. A completely deployable native app would be generated if you use mobile hybrid applications, and the application can use native components within an HTML page. It allows the SDK that includes mobile platform libraries through which you can access the native code.

After the development of the application, some advanced topics need to be covered to enhance the mobile application's functionalities to its maximum capabilities.

Push notification

Mobile OS vendors such as Apple, Google, Microsoft, and others provide a free of cost feature through which a message can be delivered to any device running on the respective OS. The OS vendors send a message commonly known as a **push message** to a device for a particular app. It is not required for an app to be running in order to receive a push message.

A push message can contain the following:

- **Alerts**: These would appear in the form of text messages
- **Badges**: These are small, circular marks on the app icon
- **Sounds**: These are audio alerts

Messages will appear in the notification center (for iOS) and notification bar (for Android). IBM Worklight provides a unified push notification architecture that simplifies sending push messages across multiple devices running on different platforms. It provides a central management console to manage mobile vendor services, for example, APNS and GCM, in the background.

Worklight provides the following push notification benefits:

- **Easy to use**: Users can easily subscribe and unsubscribe to a push service
- **Quick message delivery**: The push message gets delivered to a user's device even if the app is currently not running on the device
- **Message feedback**: It is possible to send feedback whenever a user receives and reads a push message

Device and platforms support

Currently, IBM Worklight supports push notifications on the following platforms:

- Android
- iOS
- Blackberry
- Microsoft

These OS vendors are named as push mediators in the push notification context.

Worklight push notification concepts and terminology

The following are some terms and concepts you should be familiar with:

- **Event source**: An event source is declared inside Worklight Adapter, which works as a channel to register mobile applications for push notifications. The following code snippet can be used to declare notification event source in adapter JavaScript code and must be declared as global level:

```
WL.Server.createEventSource({
    name: 'PushEventSource',
```

```
onDeviceSubscribe: 'deviceSubscribeFunc',
onDeviceUnsubscribe: 'deviceUnsubscribeFunc',
securityTest:'PushApplication-strong-mobile-securityTest'
});
```

- **Device token**: Push mediators such as Apple or Google assign a unique ID to a specific device in order to deliver messages. The Worklight server uses these IDs in order to send push messages.

- **User ID**: Worklight collects a unique ID for a specific user through authentication or other unique identifiers such as a persistent cookie.

- **Application ID**: A Worklight application ID identifies a specific Worklight application.

- **To send a notification**: The following adapter function will be used to send a push notification message. Here, the adapter function is accepting two parameters, userId and notificationText, and finding the user subscription for a particular user ID and then notifying the device by responding to the notificationText message:

```
functionsubmitNotification(userId, notificationText){
  varuserSubscription =
    WL.Server.getUserNotificationSubscription('PushAdapter.
PushEventSource', userId);

  if (userSubscription==null){
    return { result: "No subscription found for user :: " + userId
};
  }

  WL.Logger.debug("submitNotification>>userId :: " + userId + ",
text :: " + notificationText);

  WL.Server.notifyAllDevices(userSubscription, {
    badge: 1,
    sound: "sound.mp3",
    activateButtonLabel: "ClickMe",
    alert: notificationText,
    payload: {
      foo : 'bar'
    }
  });

  return { result: "Notification sent to user :: " + userId };
}
```

- **Subscribing/unsubscribing**: A mobile app needs to subscribe for an **event source** in order to receive push messages. Worklight provides the `WL.Client.Push.subscribe()` API function to register the device against a push services mediator, and in return, it collects a device token. The following code shows how to use the API function to subscribe for an event source:

```
WL.Client.Push.subscribe("myPush", {
    onSuccess: pushSubscribe_Callback,
    onFailure: pushSubscribe_Callback
});
```

In order to subscribe to a device for push service, the user must approve it first. Upon the user's approval, the device registers itself with an Apple or Google push server to obtain a token value; it also sends a subscription request to Worklight Server. All of this is automatically done by the Worklight framework.

Worklight Server stores users' subscription information in a database. It stores device IDs, token, and event source details. Unsubscribing to a device can happen in either of the two ways: either by calling the `WL.Client.Push.unsubscribe()` API function or the push mediator, which informs Worklight Server that the device is permanently not accessible. An example code to unsubscribe to a device is as follows:

```
WL.Client.Push.unsubscribe("myPush", {
    onSuccess: pushUnsubscribe_Callback,
    onFailure: pushUnsubscribe_Callback
});
```

The following figure describes how the push notification works within Worklight:

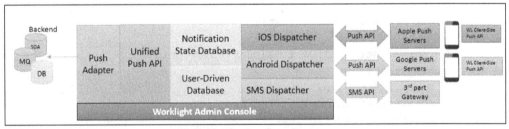

Push Notification flow diagram

 When a request to unsubscribe to a device is received by Worklight Server, it automatically clears the corresponding device token and related attributes from the push tables.

WL client API

For the native app developed using web technologies or hybrid technologies, we refer to some classes and functions that extend components such as `WL.BusyIndicator`, `WL.Logger`, and `WL.SimpleDialog` with the native look and feel, which is specified with respect to mobile platforms.

To enable these native components, Worklight provides some extensive libraries to implement. We will cover some WL client-side APIs to provide you with a holistic view of implementation at the development side.

WL.BusyIndicator

The `WL.BusyIndicator` WL extension provides a busy indicator for a mobile application. It's a modal representation of an object named `WL.BusyIndicator`. It provides a dynamic graphical interface for an application that is temporarily on hold for any process or seems busy. It appears natively on Android, iOS, Blackberry, and Windows phones. For every mobile environment, its implementation occurs by using JavaScript in the `Busy.js` file. There are some optional parameters as well.

To change the graphical appearance of the busy indicator, you can also override the defined CSS selectors: `#WLbusy`, `#WLbusyOverlay`, and `#WLbusyTitle`. Use the following code to do this:

```
varbusyIndicator = new WL.BusyIndicator('context', {text :
'Loading...'});
```

WL.Logger

The `WL.Logger` object displays log messages to the console log for every particular environment. In mobile applications, the messages are printed to a logfile provided in the mobile SDK. In web environments, the messages seem to be printed to the browser log. In desktop environments, they are printed to the applicable debug console of each environment. Refer to the details in the following section.

`WL.Logger` is an object that actually holds two methods. Both these methods contain one required parameter and one optional parameter.

The method for successful cases is as follows:

```
WL.Logger.debug("content",ex);
```

The method for errors is as follows:

```
WL.Logger.error("content",ex);
```

In the preceding methods, the optional parameter ex is a JavaScript exception. If the JavaScript exception is specified, the filename and line number are appended to the message.

WL.SimpleDialog

WL.SimpleDialog is a dialog object. It holds a common API for generating a dialog for the application. This dialog object shows a dialog box with buttons. Its appearance and specification is dependent on the environment. On Android, iPhone, BlackBerry, and Windows phones, it opens as a native dialog box. This dialog appears without any conflicts with the JavaScript thread.

The WL.SimpleDialog object's method for displaying the dialog contains four parameters in which three are mandatory and one is optional. The following is the code for the show method:

```
WL.SimpleDialog.show(title, text, buttons, options)
```

In the preceding code line, the buttons parameter is a JSON array on behalf of every corresponding button. Following is an example of a JSON array:

```
WL.SimpleDialog.show(
"Title", "Text",
[{text: "Button1", handler: function()
  {WL.Logger.debug("Button 1 pressed"); }
}]
)
```

Cordova plugins

A Cordova plugin is an open source, cross-platform mobile development architecture that allows the creation of multiplatform-deployable mobile apps. These apps can access native component features of devices using an API having web technologies such as HTML 5, JavaScript, and CSS 3. Apache Cordova Plugins are integrated into IBM Worklight Android and iOS projects. In this chapter, we will describe how Apache Cordova leverages the ability to merge the JavaScript interface as a wrapper on the web side in a native container with the device native interface on the mobile device platform.

The most critical aspect of Cordova plugins is to deal with the native functionalities such as camera, bar code scanning, contacts list, and many other native features, currently running on multiple platforms. JavaScript doesn't provide such extensibility to enhance the scripting with respect to the native devices.

In order to have a native feature's accessibility, we provide a library corresponding to the device's native feature so that JavaScript can communicate through it. When the need arises for a web page to execute the native feature functionality, the following points of access are available:

- The scenario has to be implemented in platform-specific manner, for example, in Android, iOS, or any other device

- In order to handle requests and responses between web pages and native pages, we need to communicate to/from web and native pages that are encrypted

By selecting the first option from the preceding list, we would find ourselves implementing and developing platform-dependent mobile applications. As we are in need of implementing mobile applications for a cross-platform mobile, and because it leads to provide cost-ineffective solutions, it is not a wise choice for Enterprise Mobile Development Solutions. It seems to be a really poor extensible for future enhancements and needs.

In this scenario, a developer needs to declare a custom Cordova plugin with a functionality that is not yet available in it. After creating a wrapping layer, this functionality will be used from the JavaScript code. As it is a standard-based architectural framework, Apache Cordova arrives with some extensible proficient architectures for these plugins that simplifies integration and communication with the native device code and its features. Some key plugins provided by Cordova are as follows:

- **Accelerometer**: This is a motion sensor that detects the change in movement relative to the current device's orientation

- **Camera**: This plugin takes a photo using the camera or can be used to retrieve a photo from the device's album

- **Geolocation**: This plugin allows you to detect the location information of the device in the form of latitude and longitude

We can implement or reconstruct any custom plugin if there is a need for a functionality that is not available within the prebuilt plugins. The Apache Cordova plugin consists of two different parts for Android; they are as follows:

- Java code that executes native features within the Android OS

- A JavaScript wrapper (an interface for executing Java code)

- In Java code, we need to extend the `org.apache.cordova.api.Plugin` class

- The plugin could be useable if we can override the `execute` method provided in the `org.apache.cordova.api.Plugin` class
- All plugins should be registered in the `res/xml/plugins.xml` file

Meanwhile, having an assurance for the secure requests for other external domain, every domain should be whitelisted in the file named `res/xml/cordova.xml`.

The following is the configuration code for the Cordova plugin in Java:

```
<cordova>

<access origin="https://developer.com" />

<!- allow secure requests to developer.com ->

</cordova>
```

A code wrapper for the Cordova plugin in JavaScript has the following structure:

```
CordovaCustomPlugin.prototype.executeNativeFunction
= function(SuccessCallback, FailCallback, param){..}
```

- `param`: This callback function is passed to the plugin from the web page calling Web Page
- `SuccessCallback`: This is a callback function for a successful call
- `FailCallback`: This is a callback function for an unsuccessful call

After adding a code wrapper, the plugin is added to a `windows.plugin` object:

```
cordova.addConstructor(function() {
cordova.addPlugin("cordovaCustomPlugin",
 new CordovaCustomPlugin());});
```

Besides this, in JavaScript, you can use `windows.plugin`, which can be called by the following code:

```
window.plugins.cordovaCustomPlugin.executeNativeFunction
(SuccessCallback, FailCallback, $("#Div").val());
```

Encrypted Offline Cache

Encrypted Offline Cache (EOC) is the mechanism that is used for storing the repeated and the most sensitive data, which is used in the client's application.

Encrypted Offline Cache is precisely known as EOC. It permits a flexible on-device data storage procedure for Android, iOS, BlackBerry, and Windows. This procedure provides a better alternative to the user for storing the manipulated data or the fetched response using the defined adapter data when offline and synchronizing the data for the usage of the server, which provides modifications that were completely developed when offline or without Internet connectivity. In order to dedicatedly create any mobile application for multiple platforms such as iOS and Android, consider using JSONStore rather than EOC. It seems to be much more practical to implement and is supposed to be the best practices of IBM. The JSONStore provides a mechanism to ease cryptographic procedures for encrypting forms and implementing security. PBKDF2 is a key derivation function that would act as the password to access encrypted data, which would be provided by the user. HTML5 cache can be used in EOC, which is not guaranteed to be persistent and is not a proper solution for the future updated versions of iOS.

You can also extend the utilization of JSONStore with its capable features to get the most consistent and secure on-device data storage mechanism for the client's application. Moving with the experience of using EOC, it would be much easier to implement and a way with improved persistent storage procedure for on-dive. In addition to this, the JSONStore holds an aptitude to inhabit and deploy data from custom employment of consuming an adapter on the desired server. The cache allows to use the HTML5 local storage for holding user data. As far as the storage size limit is concerned, HTML5 consumes a limit of 4 to 5 MB, which is supposed to be similar to approximately around 1.3 MB of unencrypted data. If the data appears to surpass the distinct limit, the comportment is undefined. You might experience interruption or delay in handling the data; it occurs when the data is in a huge amount and at the threshold limit.

The following exceptions can be thrown by the `WL.EncryptedCache` methods:

- `WL.EncryptedCache.ERROR_NO_EOC`: This is thrown when `create_if_none` is `false` but no encrypted cache was formerly initialized

- `WL.EncryptedCache.ERROR_LOCAL_STORAGE_NOT_SUPPORTED`: This is thrown when the HTML5 local storage interface is inaccessible

- `WL.EncryptedCache.ERROR_KEY_CREATION_IN_PROGRESS`: This is thrown when the encrypted storage is processing an open or `changeCredentials` request

- `WL.EncryptedCache.ERROR_EOC_CLOSED`: This is thrown when the encrypted cache was not appropriately initialized by using `WL.EncryptedCache`

Storage JSONStore

IBM Worklight delivers an API that does its work with JSONStore, consuming the `WL.JSONStore` class using the JavaScript-defined method. While JSONStore features allows persistent storage of **JavaScript Object Notation (JSON)** documents, as well as developer can utilize security by enabling data encryption such as **AES (Advance Encryption Standard)** with 256-bit and **PBKDF2 (Password based key Derivation Function 2)**.

JSONStore has more features over EOC and will be time saving and easy to implement approach with other benefits such as file-based storage, data encryption, integration with Worklight Adapter, indexing, JavaScript APIs for data manipulation, and fully supported in Android and iOS platform.

By means of the JSONStore API, you can encompass the functionality of the existing adapter connectivity model to store data locally and force modifications from the client to a server.

JSONStore must be initialized on application startup with the help of this `WL.JSONStore.initCollection` method with success and failure callback to make sure if the device is capable of it. For CRUD operation over storage you'll find defined method under this URL: `http://pic.dhe.ibm.com/infocenter/wrklight/v5r0m5/topic/com.ibm.worklight.help.doc/apiref/r_class_wl_jsonstore.html`.

Simply, a single occurrence of the JSON store is supported per app. However, the instance can save countless collections. A collection is associated to an adapter by requiring the adapter selection as a chunk of the collection. You do not have to subordinate a collection with an adapter; however, if an adapter is not definite for the collection, it calls `push` and `pushSelected`, which returns an error.

The following points must be kept in mind while using JSONStore for development:

- To test the JSONStore code, you must run this code on real device or emulator as it's not supported in Worklight supplied mobile browser simulator by IBM
- JSONStore is only accessible from a hybrid platform; you cannot access this data from native code
- JSON collection names must not begin with a digit or symbol
- Data encryption can be enforced without making a connection to the server
- Data storage is unlimited but limited to the device memory

Summary

At the end of this chapter, you have learned every advanced feature that IBM Worklight contains. Worklight API, push notification overview and implementation details, and concepts of offline access and encrypted cache were covered. Besides this, JSON store has the most diverse mechanism to allow local storage, and it enhances the mobile application functionalities in a much more optimum and efficient way. This chapter also provides Worklight client-side API, which is recommended by IBM as a best practice.

Index

hybrid mobile applications 49
Hypertext Markup Language (HTML) 10

I

IBM Installation Manager
  about 18
  installing 18
IBM Worklight
  environment, adding 57-60
IBM Worklight Adapter
  about 69
  communication components 70
  elements 70
  HTTP adapter 72
  HTTP adapter, creating 72-78
  Java code, calling 85-88
  Java code, invoking from adapter 88
  procedure, invoking 85
  SQL adapter 78
  SQL adapter, creating 81-84
  SQL adapters 79
  types 71
IBM Worklight application
  creating 33-36
  display, providing to mobile application
    39, 40
  previewing, in mobile simulator 46, 47
  resources 37, 38
IBM Worklight Application Center 12, 16
IBM Worklight client-side API 50
IBM Worklight Console 12, 16
IBM Worklight Consumer Edition
  installing 17
IBM Worklight Developer Edition
  installing 26, 27
IBM Worklight Device Runtime
  about 11, 14
  features 14
IBM Worklight Server
  about 11, 15
  database, configuring for 21, 22
  packages, installing 19
  structure 15
IBM Worklight solution
  about 9
  capabilities 10

components 11
  supported platforms 10
IBM Worklight Studio
  about 11, 12
  installing 25, 26

J

Java Runtime Environment. *See* JRE
JavaScript file, IBM Worklight Adapter 71
JavaScript Object Notation (JSON) 120
jQuery Mobile 9
JRE
  URL, for setup files 17
JSONStore
  about 120
  considerations, for development 120

L

Lightweight Directory Access Protocol
  (LDAP) 85
Lightweight Third Party Authentication
  (LTPA) 16
login modules
  about 94
  generating 97

M

MainLayout.xml file 67
methods, WLClient
  WL.Client.init 51
  WL.Client.invokeProcedure 51
  WL.Client.isConnected 51
  WL.Client.isUserAuthenticated 51
  WL.Client.login 51
  WL.Client.logout 51
methods, WL.EncryptedCache
  WL.EncryptedCache.ERROR_KEY_CREA-
    TION_IN_PROGRESS 119
  WL.EncryptedCache.ERROR_LOCAL_
    STORAGE_NOT_SUPPORTED 119
  WL.EncryptedCache.ERROR_NO_EOC 119
Microsoft 111
mobile application
  server configuration, verifying 43

Thank you for buying
IBM Worklight Mobile Application Development Essentials

About Packt Publishing

Packt, pronounced 'packed', published its first book "Mastering phpMyAdmin for Effective MySQL Management" in April 2004 and subsequently continued to specialize in publishing highly focused books on specific technologies and solutions.

Our books and publications share the experiences of your fellow IT professionals in adapting and customizing today's systems, applications, and frameworks. Our solution based books give you the knowledge and power to customize the software and technologies you're using to get the job done. Packt books are more specific and less general than the IT books you have seen in the past. Our unique business model allows us to bring you more focused information, giving you more of what you need to know, and less of what you don't.

Packt is a modern, yet unique publishing company, which focuses on producing quality, cutting-edge books for communities of developers, administrators, and newbies alike. For more information, please visit our website: www.packtpub.com.

About Packt Enterprise

In 2010, Packt launched two new brands, Packt Enterprise and Packt Open Source, in order to continue its focus on specialization. This book is part of the Packt Enterprise brand, home to books published on enterprise software – software created by major vendors, including (but not limited to) IBM, Microsoft and Oracle, often for use in other corporations. Its titles will offer information relevant to a range of users of this software, including administrators, developers, architects, and end users.

Writing for Packt

We welcome all inquiries from people who are interested in authoring. Book proposals should be sent to author@packtpub.com. If your book idea is still at an early stage and you would like to discuss it first before writing a formal book proposal, contact us; one of our commissioning editors will get in touch with you.

We're not just looking for published authors; if you have strong technical skills but no writing experience, our experienced editors can help you develop a writing career, or simply get some additional reward for your expertise.

PUBLISHING

PhoneGap 3 Beginner's Guide

ISBN: 978-1-78216-098-4   Paperback: 308 pages

A guide to building cross-platform apps using the W3C standards-based Cordova/PhoneGap framework

1. Understand the fundamentals of cross-platform mobile application development from build to distribution.

2. Learn to implement the most common features of modern mobile applications.

3. Take advantage of native mobile device capabilities — including the camera, geolocation, and local storage — using HTML, CSS, and JavaScript.

Mobile First Bootstrap

ISBN: 978-1-78328-579-2   Paperback: 92 pages

Develop advanced websites optimized for mobile devices using the Mobile First feature of Bootstrap

1. Get to grips with the essentials of mobile first development with Bootstrap.

2. Understand the entire process of building a mobile-first website with Bootstrap from scratch.

3. Packed with screenshots that help guide you through how to build an appealing website from a mobile-first perspective with the help of a real-world example.

Please check **www.PacktPub.com** for information on our titles